MW01611994

Reading Lessons Through Literature

Level 2

Kathy Jo DeVore

www.barefootmeandering.com

veritas • gnaritas • libertas

Table of Contents

Part 2: Spelling Lists 127

Part 3: Elson Book 1 185

Appendices   359

Quick Start

This introduction focuses on getting you started. If you want more information about the Orton-Gillingham method of reading and spelling instruction and the importance of teaching phonograms, please see Appendix A.

Reading Lessons Through Literature has three parts. Following is an overview of each part.

Part 1. Begin teaching the phonograms. There are some slight differences between Orton programs regarding which phonograms are taught. This program teaches seventy-five basic phonograms.

Part 2. After you've taught the first 26 phonograms (*a* to *z*), begin teaching the spelling words. Simple but explicit instructions are given for having children start their own spelling notebooks. Spelling rules are referred to when applicable. Children can generally learn 10-15 words per week in Kindergarten, 20 words per week in 1st grade, and 40 words per week in 2nd grade.

Part 3. After you've taught the first 200 spelling words (lists 1-A through 1-T), you can introduce the stories. Spelling lists are arranged around the stories in the Elson Readers. The stories are divided into 173 readings which correspond to the spelling lists. A child may read a story when he's learned all the words in a story and is comfortable reading the words from his spelling notebook. It is fine if he still needs to sound the words out, but he should not be struggling.

Necessary Materials

Children learn to both read and write the phonograms in this program. This can be in the optional workbook, on a white board, in a sand tray, or any other method you wish. Instructions are included later in this introduction for adapting the program for a child who is unable to learn to write while he learns to read.

Children do need a place to write spelling words. You can either print and use the blank page from the workbook or purchase a primary composition book for this notebook. Primary composition books are produced by both Mead® and Roaring Spring. If you use the blank page from the workbook, keep the spelling lists separate from the rest of the workbook. Children should read their spelling words daily, so it's best if they don't have to search for them.

Part 1: The Phonograms

Part 1 contains a page for each of the 75 basic phonograms. It is set-up with one phonogram per page in order to make flashcards unnecessary. If you prefer flashcards, a free set is available to download on my site.

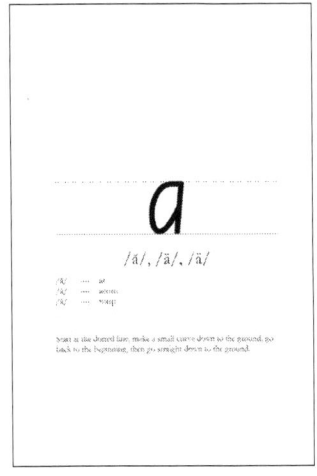

Children begin by learning the basic phonograms. Four to five year olds can learn at least two phonograms per day. Older children can often learn four per day without difficulty.

Each phonogram page has the phonogram with its sound(s) just below it. Some phonograms contain a line that lists advanced phonogram sounds—these should be skipped for new readers; see the section "Basic and Advanced Phonograms" just before the phonogram pages. After the sounds and advanced sounds is a sample word for each sound—this is for the parent, not the child.

Children should learn to read and write two new phonograms each day. The method is simple and follows a multisensory approach. Seeing, hearing, saying, and doing—these are the basics in multisensory learning. Using multiple senses to learn new information helps the brain process the information, which helps children to remember the information better and longer.

- During the oral portion of the lesson, using either the phonogram pages in this book or flashcards, have children

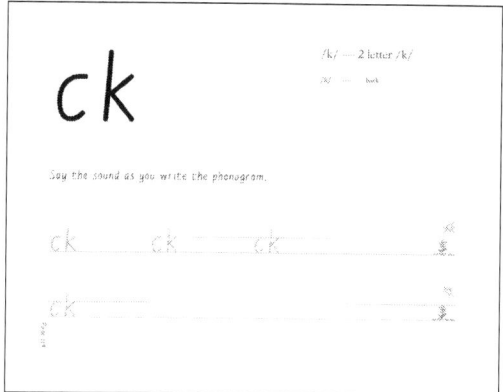
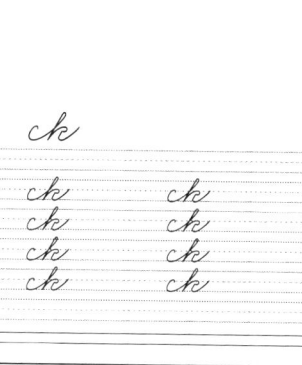

Sample phonogram pages. The left is from the optional workbook. The right is an example of how to set up a phonogram page in a primary composition book.

repeat the sound(s) of each phonogram several times while looking at it.

- Before moving to the written portion of the lesson, have children practice making the phonograms in other ways while saying the sounds. Start with large motions, having them write the phonograms in the air. Move on to smaller motions by having them use a finger to trace the phonograms, either on paper or using sandpaper letters. You can also use blocks or wooden letters.

- During the written portion of the lesson, have children say the sound(s) of each phonogram while writing it approximately six to eight times. This can be in the optional workbook, in a composition book, on a white board, in a sand tray, or any other method you wish.

Learning the phonograms, or even just the basic sounds of the twenty-six letters of the alphabet, is not a simple task. Children will forget the sounds, but that's okay. Just keep moving forward and eventually the sounds will stick. Help them with the sounds when they forget. I do this quickly while reviewing. If the child hesitates, I say the sound(s); I have the child repeat the sound(s); and I move on to the next phonogram.

Do not stop teaching new phonograms. It feels counter-intuitive, but they do not have to know the phonograms perfectly before being introduced to more phonograms or beginning spelling. In fact, using the phonograms in spelling will actually help them remember the phonograms better.

A phonogram can make up to six sounds. Sample words are given to help the instructor identify each sound, but they are for the instructors, not the children. We do not want to give children extra steps to wade through, like words or pictures, while trying to remember the sounds.

An internet search will yield audio files of the phonograms being spoken. It is important to say only the phonogram sound; remember that *b* says /b/, not /buh/. Also, it is important to teach the sounds of the letters, not the names, as only the sounds are necessary for reading. The names of the letters can be taught later. Once the sounds are firmly memorized, I begin casually referring to the letters by name instead of by their phonogram names.

While teaching, the "name" of a phonogram is the sound or sounds that the phonogram makes. However, in some cases, it includes a phrase to help differentiate one phonogram from another with the exact, or almost exact, same sound(s). The phonogram name—the sound(s) plus any identifying phrase—is what children initially learn to say when they see that phonogram. For instance, the phonogram *ck* is taught as "/k/, two letter /k/." This differentiates it from *k* which makes the same single sound.

Some phonograms are taught with an applicable spelling rule. For instance, English words do not end in the letter *i*, so the phonogram *ai* is "/ā/, two letter /ā/ that we may not use at the end of English words." After a child has learned this well, he can simply say, "/ā/, two letter /ā/," during reviews. Occasionally, ask, "May it be used at the end of English words?" as part of the review.

Once the first 26 phonograms—*a* through *z*—are learned, children will begin learning spelling words, which then eases them into reading.

Part 2: The Spelling Lists

Begin dictating spelling words after teaching all of the single letter phonograms; these are *a* to *z*, so the last single letter phonogram is z.

The spelling lists are made up of some of the most common words in the English language, but they are also arranged around the stories in the Elson Readers. Level 1 includes the stories from the Elson Readers Primer; Level 2 includes the stories from the Elson Readers Book

1—A	
top	not
but	hat
cat	bed
red	ran
six	run

1; Level 3 includes the stories from the Elson Readers Book 2; and Level 4 includes the stories from the Elson Readers Book 3.

Children can generally learn 10-15 words per week in Kindergarten, 20 words per week in 1st grade, and 40 words per week in 2nd grade. Full instructions for dictating the spelling lists are in Part 2. The following is just a basic overview.

Begin dictating 10-15 spelling words per week to the child while continuing to teach two new phonograms per day. You can dictate two or three words per day, five words two or three times per week, or any combination that works for you. For children still developing fine motor control, a few words every day can help them exercise those muscles without the stress that more writing would cause.

Children will create their own spelling notebooks. They should read their spelling words daily. The spelling lists give explicit instructions for both student and instructor, but the phonogram sounds are not listed in the spelling lists. It is assumed that the instructor will learn the phonograms the same way the student will—through repetition. Until then, I recommend printing out a copy of the list of phonograms and keeping it handy during lessons. You can download phonogram posters from our site which can be printed on regular letter paper, front and back, for a handy one-page quick reference guide.

Read each word out loud. Pronounce each word carefully, exaggerating any vowel sounds that tend to be indistinct in normal speech. Give the word phonogram by phonogram as the child writes it; have the child leave a space between syllables; and then have the child read the word aloud. Phonograms are marked according to which of their sounds they make in a given word and by which spelling rules apply to them. This is explained further in Part 2.

Part 3: The Readers

Level 1 teaches 200 spelling words (lists 1-A through 1-T) before the first story. After these words have been taught, and the child is comfortable reading them—perhaps still sounding out words, but not struggling—the stories can be introduced.

Spelling lists are arranged around the stories in the Elson Readers. Each list corresponds to the story with the same number. Part 3 in this book contains the stories from one of the Elson Readers.

In the first three levels, children will not encounter a word in their reading until they have first analyzed the word, the base word, or the word with another affix as a spelling word. Children may read a story when they have learned all the words in a story and are comfortable reading the words from their spelling notebooks. Again, it's okay if children still need to sound out the words, but they should not be struggling.

The Elson Readers include traditional stories, folk tales, and fables; stories about nature and festivals; and poetry, including Mother Goose rhymes and poems by poets such as Christina G. Rossetti and Robert Louis Stevenson. Retellings of old tales have been simplified, but not dumbed down.

I have made some changes to these classic readers. Archaic animal names have been changed to reflect the more common modern names. I've made minor changes in punctuation and wording. And finally, I've removed the majority of the pictures, usually leaving only one per story. While the original artwork by L. Kate Deal is quite charming, I believe that it's best that beginning readers do not have picture clues to the text. That can encourage guessing instead of practicing decoding skills.

Part of the philosophy behind the Lessons Through Literature programs is to help children progress in incremental steps. In the Elson Readers Primer, included in Level 1, the multi-letter phonograms are underlined and multi-syllable words are written with the syllables separated, for two reasons. First, this supports the beginning reader in reading longer words while he's still learning. Second, because some rules explain when vowels say their long sounds in syllables, seeing the syllables reinforces those rules. In the Elson Readers Book 1, included in Level 2, the stories still have multi-syllable words written with the syllables separated. And finally, in the Elson Readers Book 2, included in Level 3, the stories are written in the normal fashion. In this way, children are able to gradually move from many helps in the stories to no help at all.

Daily Tasks

You can see very general sample schedules in Part 2. More specific sample schedules are in Appendix C.

While working through Part 1:

1. Review orally all the phonograms which have been learned.

2. Learn to read and write two new phonograms. During the oral portion of the lesson, have the child say the sound(s) of each phonogram while looking at it. Air write and finger trace the phonograms. During the written portion of the lesson, have the child say the sound(s) of each phonogram while writing it. This can be in the workbook, on a white board, in a sand tray, or any other method you wish.

After you've taught all of the phonograms, review the letters of the alphabet while teaching capital letters in the same way.

3. This step is not strictly necessary, but it can be helpful. Once or twice a week, have a phonogram quiz. Call out the phonograms while the child writes them. Again, use any method of writing that you wish. If necessary, give a hint on how to

start the first letter of the phonogram, or you may show the phonogram briefly.

When you begin spelling, after learning the phonogram z:

4. Every day, read all of the spelling words already learned.

5. Dictate 10-15 new spelling words per week to the child, phonogram by phonogram. Explicit instructions are given in Part 2.

When you begin reading the stories:

6. Read, and re-read, the stories. I recommend that new readers read each story at least twice. Once the child is reading more fluently, it is enough to read each story only once. If you have a child who finds reading the same story twice more frustrating than encountering new words, by all means, skip the second reading. He may, however, find a second reading more enjoyable than just reading his spelling notebook.

Although the spelling lists are arranged around the stories in the Elson Readers, they are also padded with words from the Ayres List, a list of a thousand of the most commonly used words in the English language. Not all of the spelling words will appear in the stories.

Slowing the Pace or Taking a Break

If you take a break from new lessons, it is recommended that you continue to review the phonograms and spelling words already learned. This can be done orally in a small amount of time.

Review Rather Than Spelling Tests

The only thing necessary for teaching spelling is to teach children to analyze words and then give them plenty of practice. They do this first through the spelling lists and then later through prepared dictation (explained in Appendix B). In our household, the only way we ever review the spelling words is by reading them.

I don't believe in spelling tests. Even when we do dictation, we do prepared dictation, which allows the student time to see and study the words before writing or typing them, because when we spell a word incorrectly, the wrong answer imprints on the brain just as a correct answer does. Charlotte Mason said it well in Home Education:

> Once the eye sees a misspelt word, that image remains; and if there is also the image of the word rightly spelt, we are perplexed as to which is which. Now we see why there could not be a more ingenious way of making bad spellers than 'dictation' as it is commonly taught. Every misspelt word is an image in the child's brain not to be obliterated by the right spelling. It becomes, therefore, the teacher's business to prevent false spelling, and, if an error has been made, to hide it away, as it were, so that the impression may not become fixed (242).

Every time children spell words incorrectly, it's another block towards spelling those words correctly. I've heard people make references to this particular phenomenon my entire life, and I've seen it with my own children. It is best to not see incorrectly spelled words while one is still learning. I tried a spelling program only once before discovering the O-G method. My oldest son had a proofreading exercise. At the end of it, after seeing words spelled incorrectly, he was no longer able to spell the words which he could previously spell without difficulty.

For my very visual firstborn, seeing words spelled incorrectly was enough. Consider that when a child spells a word incorrectly on a spelling test, he is using multiple senses. He is seeing the word and writing it down. In practice tests, he has likely spelled the word incorrectly out loud as well. Everything you hear about multisensory learning works in reverse as well.

The only point to a spelling test is to inform the instructor of the child's ability. Please consider that for a moment. Think carefully on this. A spelling test has absolutely no benefit to the child. For the child who is struggling with spelling, by placing those incorrectly spelled words in the child's mind, the spelling test has actually become a stumbling block to correct spelling. But even the child who has no trouble with spelling has not benefitted from the exercise.

Young children who are fairly new readers are still internalizing spelling, from their reading and also from explicit spelling instruction. I leave this process alone to work slowly in the background. I do not test to see if it's working.

In our household, here's how this plays out: I don't put my children in a position to fail while they're still going through this process. That means that I do not require original written work from my children in the early grades. They do copywork. They do oral narrations, which I write for them. I don't prevent them from doing their own writing, but I never require it. By the time I begin requiring writing from them, when they begin doing their own written narrations and prepared dictations around 3rd or 4th grade, they're ready for them.

For those who really feel the need to do more with the spelling lists with younger children, you can use our optional copywork book which includes the entire text of the Elson Readers Primer. This is the path that I recommend.

Non-Writers

Some children have problems which prevent them from learning to write, but they are ready to learn to read. My older three boys all learned to read without a writing component to their lessons. So, while I do believe the writing helps, I also recognize that it's not strictly necessary to learn to read. I hope these instructions will help you adapt the program if you have a child who cannot do the writing portion.

When you introduce the phonograms, simply skip the writing portion of the lesson. If possible, work on letter formation through air writing or finger tracing the letters.

When it is time to begin the spelling lists, use phonogram flashcards or tiles; both are available as free downloads from our website. It's important to use something with phonograms, not letters, because we want children thinking in terms of phonograms rather than individual letters. Make sure that you have enough cards or tiles to complete each word in the list. As you dictate each word (explained more fully in Part 2), have children identify each phonogram as you call it out and put the phonograms together to form the word. Then, write the word in the spelling book and have the child mark it as much as possible. Alternatively, explain the markings as you make them. Later, have the child tell you how to mark the words.

Using Reading Lessons as a Spelling Program

Once children have begun to read fluently, you can focus on using Reading Lessons Through Literature as a spelling program rather than a reading instruction program.

While children are learning to read, instructors might dictate as many as 40-50 words per week, depending on the ages of the children. However, as a spelling program, you can slow the pace down to 10-20 words per week and spend more time on reading. A good goal after attaining reading fluency is to complete one level of Reading Lessons per school year. Using Reading Lessons in this way provides a prolonged period of study and practice with the phonograms and spelling rules. This will continue to reinforce what the child has already learned while keeping his skills sharp until he is old enough to begin prepared dictation.

If you are beginning Reading Lessons as a spelling program with an older, fluent reader, I recommend going through Level 1 at a quick pace before slowing down to one level per school year.

Because Reading Lessons is based on practice and repetition, I do recommend that everyone starts in Level 1. The student may already know how to spell all of the words, but if he's new to analyzing words, it will be helpful to begin with the easiest words. The exception is for people who have some experience with an O-G program which utilizes phonograms and marks spelling words. If you have this experience and are strongly opposed to starting at Level 1, I recommend Level 2. It is important to note that children learn all 75 phonograms in Level 1, so the lists in Level 2 assume that the student already knows all the phonograms.

Struggling Spellers

For older students who struggle with spelling, a more intense course of study may be necessary. The spelling lists in Reading Lessons include the complete Ayres List—1,000 of the most common words in English as compiled by Leonard Ayres in the early 1900s—in addition to the 1,500 other words necessary to read the stories. Mastering these words will give students a good foundation.

To accomplish this, you can go through the books at a faster pace, multiple times. For instance, dictate 30-50 words per week. Complete Levels 1 and 2 at this pace, then start over with Level 2. Complete Levels 2 and 3, then start over with Level 3. Continue until you have gone through each book twice.

In addition to the spelling words, use the readers—once these words have been analyzed by the student—for copywork. You can also add prepared copywork: Choose a copywork passage and have the student analyze several words from the passage before copying it. When the student is ready, begin prepared dictation (explained in Appendix B).

Stay the Course

A new homeschooling mother asked, "Which reading program will teach my child to read?" An experienced homeschooling mother replied, "The third one."

Sometimes, we change curricula because we read new research or we learn new information, so we change to a program that is better or better fits our own educational philosophy. But other times, we simply don't give a program time to work. Learning to read takes time, and it also relies on the developmental readiness of the child. If the methodology behind a program is sound, then there is no reason to switch programs. Reading is hard work and requires lots of practice. Whatever program you use, give it time to work.

Part 1

Phonograms & Spelling Rules

Basic and Advanced Phonograms

Advanced phonograms are ones which are uncommon or which appear in more advanced words. In addition to the advanced phonograms, some of the basic phonograms have advanced sounds.

I recommend teaching only the basic sounds of the basic phonograms to new readers to simplify matters for them. Older students may learn the advanced sounds of the basic phonograms as well as the advanced phonograms, **but keep in mind that many words with advanced phonograms can also be explained with silent letters or as exceptions**. You may never feel the need to teach the advanced phonograms at all.

The phonogram pages for the basic phonograms show both basic and advanced phonogram sounds when applicable, formatted as in the sample. The advanced phonograms appear after the 75 basic phonograms; each of these pages has "Advanced Phonogram" at the top of the page. I have included them here both for the convenience of those who choose to teach them and also to make these pages a good reference guide for all stages of learning.

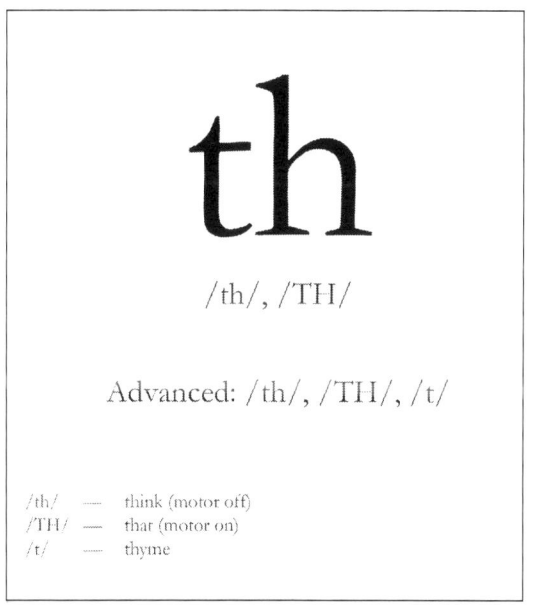

Some of the basic phonograms have advanced sounds. In the 75 Basic Phonograms list, only the basic sounds are listed, but the phonograms with advanced sounds have an asterisk (*) next to them. In the Advanced Phonograms list, the phonograms are listed with all of their sounds, basic and advanced, and the phonograms with basic sounds have an asterisk (*) next to them.

75 Basic Phonograms

a	/ă/, /ā/, /ä/	at, acorn, wasp
b	/b/	but
c	/k/, /s/	cat, city
d	/d/	dog
e	/ĕ/, /ē/	best, me
f	/f/	four
g	/g/, /j/	garden, gem
h	/h/	hat
i	/ĭ/, /ī/, /ē/, /y/	igloo, ice, radio, onion
j	/j/	jam
k	/k/	kite
l	/l/	lot
m	/m/	mat
n	/n/	no
o	/ŏ/, /ō/, /oo/	pot, go, to
p	/p/	put
qu	/kw/	queen
r	/r/	run
s	/s/, /z/	sass, has
t	/t/	tap
u	/ŭ/, /ū/, /ü/	umbrella, unit, put
v	/v/	vowel
w	/w/	water
x	/ks/	fox
y	/y/, /ĭ/, /ī/, /ē/	yellow, gym, sky, baby
z *	/z/	zoo
ai *	/ā/ — 2 letter /ā/ we may NOT use at the end of English words	hail
ar	/är/	car
au *	/ä/ — 2 letter /ä/ that we may NOT use at the end of English words	pauper
augh	/ä/, /af/	caught, laugh
aw	/ä/ — 2 letter /ä/ that we MAY use at the end of English words	paw
ay *	/ā/ — 2 letter /ā/ that we MAY use at the end of English words	play
bu	/b/ — 2 letter /b/	build
ch	/ch/, /k/, /sh/	church, Christ, chef
cei	/sē/	receive

ci	/sh/ — short /sh/ ("short" because it begins with a short letter)	facial
ck	/k/ — 2 letter /k/	back
dge	/j/ — 3 letter /j/	dodge
ea	/ē/, /ĕ/, /ā/	beat, dread, break
ear	/er/ as in pearl	pearl
ed	/ed/, /d/, /t/	waded, slammed, picked
ee	/ē/ — double /ē/	tee
ei *	/ā/, /ē/, /ī/	their, protein, feisty
eigh	/ā/, /ī/	eight, height
er	/er/ as in her	her
ew	/oo/, /ū/	dew, few
ey *	/ā/, /ē/	they, key
gn	/n/ — 2 letter /n/ that we use at the beginning or the end of a word	gnome, sign
gu	/g/, /gw/	guest, language
ie	/ē/ — 2 letter /ē/	thief
igh	/ī/ — 3 letter /ī/	sight
ir	/er/ as in dirt	dirt
kn	/n/ — 2 letter /n/ that we use only at the beginning of a base word	know
mb	/m/ — 2 letter /m/	comb
ng	/ng/	ding (nasal sound)
oa	/ō/ — 2 letter /ō/	boat
oe *	/ō/, /oo/	doe, shoe
oi	/oi/ that we may NOT use at the end of English words	toil
oo	/oo/, /ü/, /ō/	food, hook, floor
or	/or/	cord
ou	/ow/, /ō/, /oo/, /ŭ/, /ü/	our, four, tour, famous, could
ough	/ŏ/, /ō/, /oo/, /ow/, /uff/, /off/	bought, dough, through, bough, rough, cough
ow	/ow/, /ō/	plow, bow
oy	/oi/ that we MAY use at the end of English words	toy
ph	/f/ — 2 letter /f/	phonics
sh	/sh/	shell
si	/sh/, /zh/	transgression, vision
tch	/ch/	clutch
th *	/th/, /TH/	think, that
ti	/sh/ — tall /sh/ ("tall" because it begins with a tall letter)	nation
ui	/oo/	fruit
ur	/er/ as in turn	turn
wh	/wh/	wheel
wor	/wer/	worm
wr	/r/ — 2 letter /r/	wreck

Advanced Phonograms

ae	/ā/, /ē/, /ĕ/	aerial, algae, aesthetic
ah	/ä/	blah
ai *	/ā/, /ī/, /ă/	mail, aisle, plaid
au *	/ä/, /ō/, /ā/, /ow/	pauper, chauffeur, gauge, sauerkraut
ay *	/ā/, /ī/	day, cayenne
cc	/ch/	cappuccino
ce	/sh/	ocean
cu	/k/, /kw/	biscuit, cuisine
eau	/ō/, /ū/, /ŏ/	bureau, beauty, bureaucracy
ei *	/ā/, /ē/, /ī/, /ĭ/, /ĕ/	their, protein, feisty, forfeit, heifer
et	/ā/	ballet
eu	/oo/, /ū/	neutral, feud
ey *	/ā/, /ē/, /ī/	they, turkey, geyser
ge	/j/, /zh/	surgeon, mirage
gh	/g/	ghost
oe *	/ō/, /oo/, /ē/	toe, shoe, subpoena
ot	/ō/	depot
our	/er/	journey
pn	/n/	pneumonia
ps	/s/	psalm
pt	/t/	pterodactyl
rh	/r/	rhyme
sc	/s/	science
sci	/ch/	conscience
th *	/th/, /TH/, /t/	thought, them, thyme
ut	/ū/	debut
yr	/ēr/, /er/	lyric, syrup
z *	/z/, /s/	zoo, quartz

30 Spelling Rules

Vowel and Vowel Sound Rules

1. **Q** always needs **u**, and **u** is not a vowel here.
2. **C** says /s/ before **e**, **i**, and **y**. Otherwise, **c** says /k/: picnic, picnicking.
3. **G** may say /j/ before **e**, **i**, and **y**. Otherwise, **g** says /g/.
4. Vowels **a**, **e**, **o**, **u** usually say /ā, ē, ō, ū/ at the end of a syllable.
5. Vowels **y** and **i** may say /ĭ/, /ī/, or /ē/ at the end of a syllable.
6. Vowel **y** says /ī/ at the end of a one-syllable word: by, sky, why.
7. Vowel **y** says /ē/ only at the end of a multi-syllable word: baby, candy.
8. Vowels **i** and **o** may say /ī/ and /ō/ when followed by two consonants.
9. At the end of a base word, /ā/ is usually spelled **ay**. There are ten exceptions when /ā/ is spelled **ey**: convey, hey, ley, obey, osprey, prey, purvey, survey, they, whey.
10. At the end of words, vowel **a** says its third sound: ma, zebra.
11. The **gh** phonograms **augh**, **ough**, **igh**, and **eigh** can each be used only at the end of a base word or before the letter **t**. The **gh** is either silent or it says /f/.

End of Base Word Rules

12. Engish words do not end in **i**, **u**, **v**, or **j**, but YOU and I are special.
13. Phonograms **dge** and **ck** are used only after a single vowel which says its short sound.
14. Phonogram **tch** is used only after a single vowel which does not say its long sound.
   Phonogram **tch** is the phonogram usually used to say /ch/ following a single vowel at the end of base words, but **ch** says /ch/ after a single vowel at the end of six base words: attach, spinach, rich, which, much, such. Phonogram **ch** is used at the end of base words following two vowels (teach, preach) and after a vowel followed by a consonant (church, bunch).
15. We often double **f**, **l**, and **s** after a single vowel at the end of a base word. We sometimes double other letters.

5 Reasons for Final Silent E

16. (1) The vowel says its name because of the **e**.
17. (2) English words do not end in **v** or **u**.
18. (3) The **e** makes **c** say /s/ or **g** say /j/.
19. (4) Every syllable must have a written vowel.
20. (5) Miscellaneous silent **e** covers all other silent **e** usages. This can include preventing a word that would otherwise end in **s** from looking plural, making a word appear larger, making **th** say /TH/, and making homonyms appear different.

Affix Rules

21. When added to another syllable, the prefix all- and the suffix -full each drop an **l**: almost, truthful.
22. When adding a vowel suffix, drop the final silent **e** unless it is still necessary according to other spelling rules, such as making **c** say /s/ or **g** say /j/: charge, chargeable, charging.
23. When adding a vowel suffix to a word ending in one vowel followed by one consonant, double the last letter only if the word is one syllable or the last syllable is accented: begin, beginning; worship, worshiping. Do not double **x**, **w**, or **y**.
24. The single vowel **y** (not part of a multi-letter phonogram) changes to **i** before adding any ending unless the ending begins with **i**: happy, happiness; try, tries, trying. This is because...
25. English words cannot have two letters **i** in a row.
26. To form the past tense of regular verbs, add **ed**. **Ed** forms a new syllable when the base word ends in the sound /d/ or /t/. Otherwise, **ed** says /d/ or /t/.
27. Use **s** to make regular nouns plural and to make the third person singular form of a regular verb. Use **es** after phonograms that hiss: **s**, **ch**, **sh**, **x**, and **z**. Refer to rule 23 when adding **es**. **Ch** does not hiss when it says /k/: stomach, stomachs.

Spelling Sh Rules

28. **Sh** spells /sh/ at the begininning of words and at the end of syllables. It never spells /sh/ at the beginning of any syllable after the first one except for the ending —ship: she, fish, hardship.
29. **Ti**, **si**, and **ci** say /sh/ at the beginning of any syllable except the first one. Look to the root word to determine which one to use: par**t**, par**ti**al; transgres**s**, transgres**si**on; fa**ce**, fa**ci**al.

Miscellaneous Rule

30. **Z** says /z/ at the beginning of a base word, never **s**.

C

/k/, /s/

/k/ — cat
/s/ — city

a

/ă/, /ā/, /ä/

/ă/ — at
/ā/ — acorn
/ä/ — wasp

d

/d/

/d/ — dog

g

/g/, /j/

/g/ — garden
/j/ — gem

O

/ŏ/, /ō/, /oo/

/ŏ/ — pot
/ō/ — go
/oo/ — to

qu

/kw/, /k/

/kw/ — queen
/k/ — croquet

i

/ĭ/, /ī/, /ē/, /y/

/ĭ/   —   igloo
/ī/   —   ice
/ē/   —   radio
/y/   —   onion

These sounds are the same as those of *y*, only the order is different. To improve memory retention, chant:

/ĭ/, /ī/, /ē/   [pause]   /y/

j

/j/

/j/ — jam

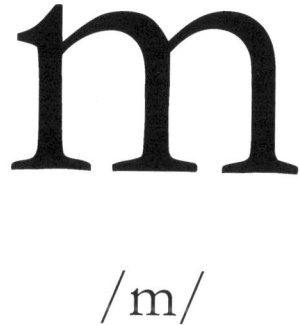

/m/

/m/ — mat

n

/n/

/n/ — no

/r/

/r/ — run

1

/l/

/l/ — lot

h

/h/

/h/ — hat

k

/k/

/k/ — kite

b

/b/

/b/   —   but

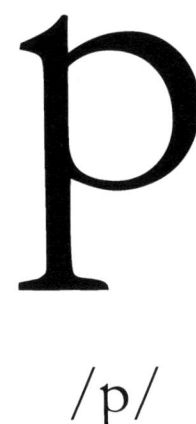

/p/

/p/ — put

t

/t/

/t/ — tap

u

/ŭ/, /ū/, /ü/

/ŭ/ — umbrella
/ū/ — unit
/ü/ — put

/y/, /ĭ/, /ī/, /ē/

/y/	—	yellow
/ĭ/	—	gym
/ī/	—	sky
/ē/	—	baby

These sounds are the same as those of *i*, only the order is different. To improve memory retention, chant:

/y/   [pause]   /ĭ/, /ī/, /ē/

e

/ĕ/, /ē/

/ĕ/ — best
/ē/ — me

/f/

/f/ — four

S

/s/ , /z/

/s/	—	sass
/z/	—	has

[Note: The second sound for **s** is /z/. However, the sounds are so similar that students will automatically adjust to the correct pronunciation for the word that they are reading, so it is possible to just teach the first sound.}

/v/

/v/ — vowel

/w/

/w/ — water

X

/ks/, /z/

/ks/ — fox
/z/ — xylophone

Z

/z/

Advanced: /z/, /s/

/z/ — zoo
/s/ — quartz

[Note: The advanced sound of **z** is /s/. However, the sounds are so similar that students will automatically adjust to the correct pronunciation for the word that they are reading, so it is possible to just teach the basic sound.]

Begin Part 2.

th

/th/, /TH/

Advanced: /th/, /TH/, /t/

/th/ — think (motor off)
/TH/ — that (motor on)
/t/ — thyme

[Note: The second sound of **th** is /TH/. However, the sounds are so similar that students will automatically adjust to the correct pronunciation for the word that they are reading, so it is possible to just teach the first sound.]

ck

/k/ — 2 letter /k/

/k/ — back

ai

/ā/ — 2 letter /ā/ that we may NOT use at the end of English words

Advanced: /ā/, /ī/, /ă/

/ā/	—	hail
/ī/	—	aisle
/ă/	—	plaid

/ā/ — 2 letter /ā/ that we MAY
use at the end of English words

Advanced: /ā/, /ī/

/ā/   —   play
/ī/   —   cayenne

sh

/sh/

/sh/ — shell

ng

/ng/

/ng/ — ding (nasal sound)

ee

/ē/ — double /ē/

/ē/ — tee

Oo

/oo/, /ü/, /ō/

/oo/ — food
/ü/ — hook
/ō/ — floor

ou

/ow/, /ō/, /oo/, /ŭ/, /ü/

/ow/ — our
/ō/   — four
/oo/ — tour
/ŭ/   — famous

/ü/   — could, should, would

[Note: Although the /ü/ sound occurs only in the above three base words, it is included in order to avoid making these common base words exceptions.]

OW

/ow/, /ō/

/ow/ — plow
/ō/ — bow

ar

/är/

/är/ — car

ch

/ch/, /k/, /sh/

/ch/ — church
/k/ — chasm
/sh/ — chef

au

/ä/ — 2 letter /ä/ that we may NOT
use at the end of English words

Advanced: /ä/, /ō/, /ā/, /ow/

/ä/   —   pauper
/ō/   —   chauffeur
/ā/   —   gauge
/ow/ —   sauerkraut

aw

/ä/ — 2 letter /ä/ that we MAY
use at the end of English words

/ä/   —   paw

Oi

/oi/ that we may NOT use at
the end of English words

/oi/ — toil

oy

/oi/ that we MAY use at the
end of English words

/oi/   —   toy

/er/ as in h<u>er</u>

/er/   —   her

The four spellings of /er/: Oyst<u>er</u>s t<u>ur</u>n d<u>ir</u>t into p<u>ear</u>ls.

M<u>er</u>maids t<u>ur</u>n and tw<u>ir</u>l with p<u>ear</u>ls.

/er/ as in t<u>ur</u>n

/ur/ — turn

The four spellings of /er/: Oyst<u>er</u>s t<u>ur</u>n d<u>ir</u>t into p<u>ear</u>ls.

M<u>er</u>maids t<u>ur</u>n and tw<u>ir</u>l with p<u>ear</u>ls.

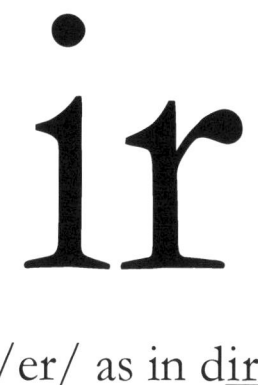

/er/ as in d<u>ir</u>t

/er/ — dirt

The four spellings of /er/: Oyst<u>er</u>s t<u>ur</u>n d<u>ir</u>t into p<u>ear</u>ls.

M<u>er</u>maids t<u>ur</u>n and tw<u>ir</u>l with p<u>ear</u>ls.

ear

/er/ as in p<u>ear</u>l

/er/ — pearl

The four spellings of /er/: Oyst<u>er</u>s t<u>ur</u>n d<u>ir</u>t into p<u>ear</u>ls.

M<u>er</u>maids t<u>ur</u>n and tw<u>ir</u>l with p<u>ear</u>ls.

wor

/wer/

/wer/ — worm

wh

/wh/

/wh/ — wheel

ea

/ē/, /ĕ/, /ā/

/ē/ — beat
/ĕ/ — bread
/ā/ — break

or

/or/

/or/   —   cord

/ed/, /d/, /t/

/ed/	—	waded
/d/	—	washed
/t/	—	picked

[Note: **Ed** is the ending used to form the past tense of regular verbs. **Ed** forms a new syllable when the base word ends in **d** or **t**. Otherwise, **ed** says /d/ or /t/.]

ew

/oo/, /ū/

/oo/ — dew
/ū/ — few

cei

/sē/

/sē/ — receive

gu

/g/, /gw/

/g/ — guest
/gw/ — language

/r/ — 2 letter /r/

/r/   —   wreck

augh

/ä/, /ăf/

/ä/ — caught
/ăf/ — laugh

ui

/oo/

/oo/ — fruit

oa

/ō/ — 2 letter /ō/

/ō/ — boat

/f/ — 2 letter /f/

/f/ — phonics

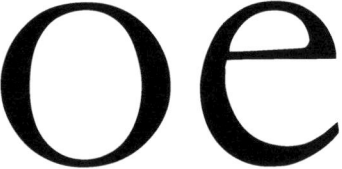

/ō/, /oo/

Advanced: /ō/, /oo/, /ē/

/ō/ — doe
/oo/ — shoe
/ē/ — subpoena

tch

/ch/

/ch/ — clutch

dge

/j/ — 3 letter /j/

/j/   —   dodge

/ā/, /ē/

Advanced: /ā/, /ē/, /ī/

/ā/	—	they
/ē/	—	key
/ī/	—	geyser

bu

/b/ — 2 letter /b/

/bu/ — build

ei

/ā/, /ē/, /ī/

Advanced: /ā/, /ē/, /ī/, /ĭ/, /ĕ/

/ā/	—	their
/ē/	—	protein
/ī/	—	feisty
/ĭ/	—	forfeit
/ĕ/	—	heifer

eigh

/ā/, /ī/

/ā/	—	eight
/ī/	—	height

ci

/sh/ — short /sh/

"short" because it begins with a short letter

/sh/ — facial

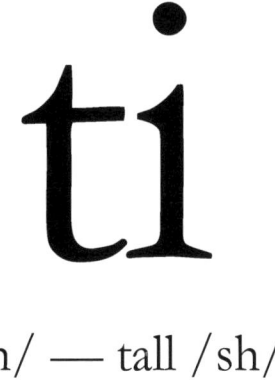

/sh/ — tall /sh/

"tall" because it begins with a tall letter

/sh/   —   nation

si

/sh/, /zh/

/sh/ — transgression
/zh/ — vision

kn

/n/ — 2 letter /n/ that we use only at
the beginning of a base word

/n/   —   know

igh

/ī/ — 3 letter /ī/

/ī/   —   sight

ie

/ē/ — 2 letter /ē/

/ē/ — thief

gn

/n/ — 2 letter /n/ that we can use at the beginning or the end of a word

/gn/ — gnarl, sign

ough

/ŏ/, /ō/, /oo/,
/ow/, /ŭff/, /ŏff/

/ŏ/   —   bought
/ō/   —   dough
/oo/   —   through
/ow/   —   bough
/ŭff/   —   rough
/ŏff/   —   cough

mb

/m/ — 2 letter /m/

/m/ — comb

Advanced Phonogram

ae

/ā/, /ē/, /ĕ/

/ā/	—	aerial
/ē/	—	algae
/ĕ/	—	aesthetic

Advanced Phonogram

ah

/ä/

/ä/   —   blah

Advanced Phonogram

cc

/ch/

/ch/ — cappuccino

Advanced Phonogram

ce

/sh/

/sh/ — ocean

Advanced Phonogram

cu

/k/, /kw/

/k/ — biscuit
/kw/ — cuisine

eau

/ō/, /ū/, /ŏ/

/ō/ — bureau
/ū/ — beauty
/ŏ/ — bureaucracy

Advanced Phonogram

et

$/\bar{a}/$

$/\bar{a}/$ — ballet

Advanced Phonogram

eu

/oo/, /ū/

/oo/ — neutral
/ū/ — feud

Advanced Phonogram

/j/, /zh/

/j/ — surgeon
/zh/ — mirage

Advanced Phonogram

gh

/g/

/g/   —   ghost

Advanced Phonogram

ot

/ō/

/ō/   —   depot

Advanced Phonogram

our

/er/

/er/ — journey

Advanced sentences for the five spellings of /er/:

Oysters turn dirt into pearls courageously.

Mermaids turn and twirl on an earthly journey.

Advanced Phonogram

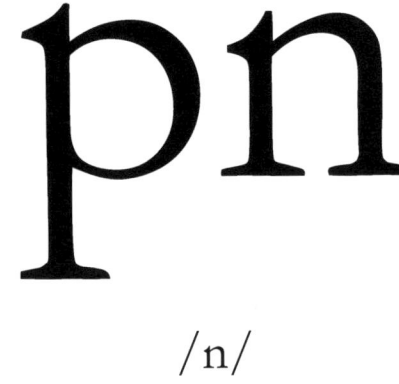

/n/

/n/ — pneumonia

Advanced Phonogram

/s/

/s/ — psalm

Advanced Phonogram

/t/

/t/ — pterodactyl

Advanced Phonogram

/r/

/r/ — rhyme

Advanced Phonogram

SC

/s/

/s/ — science

Advanced Phonogram

sci

/ch/

/ch/ — conscience

Advanced Phonogram

/ū/

/ū/ — debut

Advanced Phonogram

yr

/ēr/, /er/

/ēr/, /er/ — lyric, syrup

Part 2

Spelling Lists

The Spelling Lists

The spelling lists are made up of some of the most common words in the English language, and they are arranged around the stories in The Elson Readers.

The child will be creating his own spelling notebook. You can either print and use the blank page from the optional workbook or purchase a primary composition book. Primary composition books are produced by both Mead® and Roaring Spring. The following pages give an overview of making the spelling notebook, and the spelling lists give explicit instructions for both student and instructor. Each word is read aloud, then given to the child phonogram by phonogram until he has completed the word. He then reads the word aloud. Phonograms are marked according to which of their sounds they make in a given word and by which spelling rules apply to them.

With five year old, Kindergarten age children, dictate 10-15 new words each week while continuing to teach two new phonograms per day. This can be five words two or three times per week, but if the child has trouble writing five words per day, dictate two to three new words every day.

With six to seven year old, first grade age children, dictate 20 new words to the child each week. This can be five words, four days per week, or it could be ten words twice a week.

Seven to eight year old, second grade children, can handle 40 to 50 words per week, ten words four or five days a week.

If you take a break, continue reviewing the phonograms and spelling words already covered.

In addition to the phonograms, there are also 30 spelling rules. The spelling rules are mentioned when applicable to a spelling word.

The next two pages give sample schedules and sample spelling notebook pages.

Monday	Tuesday	Wednesday	Thursday	Friday
Review Phonograms	Review Phonograms	Phonogram Quiz	Review Phonograms	Phonogram Quiz
Learn 2 New Phonograms	Learn 2 New Phonograms	Learn 2 New Phonograms	Learn 2 New Phonograms	Learn 2 New Phonograms
Read Spelling Words	Read Spelling Words	Read Spelling Words	Read Spelling Words	Read Spelling Words
Dictate 2-3 New Spelling Words	Dictate 2-3 New Spelling Words	Dictate 2-3 New Spelling Words	Dictate 2-3 New Spelling Words	Dictate 2-3 New Spelling Words

Monday	Tuesday	Wednesday	Thursday	Friday
Review Phonograms	Review Phonograms	Phonogram Quiz	Review Phonograms	Phonogram Quiz
Learn 2 New Phonograms	Learn 2 New Phonograms	Learn 2 New Phonograms	Learn 2 New Phonograms	Learn 2 New Phonograms
Read Spelling Words	Read Spelling Words	Read Spelling Words	Read Spelling Words	Read Spelling Words
Dictate 5 New Spelling Words		Dictate 5 New Spelling Words		(Optional) Dictate 5 New Spelling Words

I-A	I-B
top	and
but	$\overset{3}{\text{all}}$
cat	$\overset{3}{\text{tall}}$
red	am
six	b<u>e</u>
not	<u>a</u>
hat	an
bed	<u>$\overset{2}{\text{the}}$</u>
ran	$\overset{2}{\text{is}}$
run	$\overset{2}{\text{has}}$

I-A

top   not

but   hat

cat   bed

red   ran

six   run

Analyzing the Spelling Words

We use markings to analyze the spelling words. All of these markings are shown and explained next to the spelling words in the lists. You do not have to know and understand all of the markings in advance. Following are some of the most common markings used. The first two have a note included in the first twenty reading lists; after that, the word is simply marked. Notes in brackets [ ] are for the instructor, not the child.

Numbers 6 through 9 are based on spelling rules, so their markings are a bit different than the ones mentioned in 1 through 5. Since the words are marked and explained for you in the spelling lists, these are merely explanations for the markings you will see rather than a list that you need to memorize.

1. Leave a space between syllables.

fish er

2. When a phonogram does not say its first sound, put a small number above it to show which sound it makes.

3
all

3. Underline multi-letter phonograms.

fi<u>sh</u>

4. Double underline silent letters. The most common is the final silent *e* at the end of words. Final silent *e* has different functions, and these functions are often marked and discussed with the word. For instance, reason 1 silent *e* makes a vowel say its name, so a bridge is drawn from the silent *e* to the vowel instead of a number 2 over the vowel.

mine

The other reasons for silent *e* are marked with a number beside the double underline and discussed with the word. All the reasons for a final silent *e* are listed in the 30 Spelling Rules at the beginning of this book. Reason 5 is a miscellaneous silent *e*, but the others have specific reasons.

<u>are</u>₌₅   Double underline the silent *e*.

5. Mark eXceptions, phonograms which don't say any of their normal sounds, with an X.

X
of

6. Underline *c* and *g* when they say /s/ and /j/ when followed by *e*, *i*, or *y*. This is a spelling rule, so the consonant receives an underline instead of a number 2 over it.

<u>c</u>ir cle   <u>g</u>erm

7. Underline *a*, *e*, *i*, *o*, and *u* when they say /ā/, /ē/, /ī/, /ō/, and /ū/ at the end of a syllable. This is a spelling rule, so the vowel receives an underline instead of a number 2 over it.

m<u>e</u>

8. Underline *i* and *o* when they say /ī/ and /ō/ when followed by two consonants. This is a spelling rule, so the vowel receives an underline instead of a number 2 over it.

c<u>o</u>lt

9. Underline *y* when it says /ī/ at the end of a one-syllable word or /ē/ at the end of a multi-syllable word. These are spelling rules, so the vowel receives an underline instead of a number over it.

sk<u>y</u>   can d<u>y</u>

Dictating the Spelling Words

1. Say the word, then say the word in a sentence if necessary or desired. I only make up a sentence when my child doesn't understand the word or when the word is a homonym.

2. Call the word out phonogram by phonogram. Give the child time to write each phonogram. Correct as necessary. If the child can't remember a phonogram, give a reminder. A white board is handy for this, but you could also use a flashcard, the phonogram pages at the front of this book, or just a sheet of paper.

For example:

top	Top. The first phonogram is /t/. The next phonogram is /ŏ/, /ō/, /oo/. The last phonogram is /p/. /t/-/ŏ/-/p/. Top.
3 all	The first phonogram is /ă/, /ā/, /ä/. Write a small 3 above it to show that it says its third sound. The next phonogram is /l/. The last phonogram is /l/. We often double /l/ after a single vowel at the end of a base word. /ä/-/l/-/l/. All.
be	The first phonogram is /b/. The next phonogram is /ĕ/, /ē/. Underline /ē/; *e* says /ē/ at the end of a syllable.

3. Have the child read the word.

Follow this format every time. After the first few words, only the additional information, such as the markings and references to spelling rules, are included.

It's important to note that this program is built upon repetition and practice. Applicable spelling rules are given with the spelling words. Over time, instructor and student will both learn these rules just from hearing and saying them so often during spelling dictation.

As you both become more comfortable with the procedure, it is also a good practice to ask the child questions to get him analyzing the words. For example:

Instructor: Is *a* making its first, second, or third sound?

Student: Second.

Instructor: It's making its second sound, so write a small 2 above it.

Instructor: Why do we need the silent *e*?

Student: Silent *e* makes *i* say /ī/.

Instructor: Double underline the silent *e*, then draw a bridge between the silent *e* and *i*.

Reading the Spelling Words

Children should read their spelling words frequently. That means daily at first. Once children have 200 words—lists 1-A through 1-T— they can begin reading the stories. At that point, you might alternate. Twice a week, children can read the new story, and on the other days, they can read their spelling words.

Once the list reaches 250 to 300 words, the list can be split into parts. For instance, have the child read the most recent 100 words, and then review 50-100 older words. We separate the spelling book with Post-it® Tabs for the sake of simplicity.

The important part is to have the child continue practicing by reading the spelling book daily. The number of words may differ between children depending on age and ability.

Sounding Out and Lazy Vowels

Some words are exceptions. This means that one of its phonograms does not make any of its normal sounds. We (sometimes) mark these phonograms with an X, but that does not help children remember the sound. I have had my children sound them out as if the word was regular. This gives them an audio clue.

As an example, let's look at the word one. When children learn one on the spelling list, we tell them, "Think to spell /ōn/." Later, when they come across it on the spelling list, we might say, "This phonogram is an exception, but sound it out as if silent *e* were making *o* say /ō/, /ō-n/. That's how the word used to be pronounced, but now we say /won/."

We can also teach that these exception words have two names, their real names and a nickname. We sound out the real name, but we call them by their nicknames.

In the first 127 spelling lists, there are 1,720 words and less than ten exceptions. I actively avoid marking exceptions because it seems that children have an easier time remembering the "nickname" after sounding the word out according to the rules rather than trying to remember what can easily become a sight word with no clues at all.

We do something similar with vowels. In English, the schwa /ə/ is the most common vowel sound. This is the common sound of a vowel in an unstressed syllable, pronounced similar to a short *u* sound—/ŭ/.

Since this information is a bit over the head of the average five year old, we can explain it by describing these vowels as lazy. The word alone is listed in the spelling list like this:

a lone   Underline /ā/ to show that it's saying /ā/ at the end of a syllable. *O* says /ō/ because of the silent *e*. Double underline the silent *e*, and draw a bridge between the *o* and the *e*.

When we sound out the word, or "think to spell," we stress the /ā/ sound, but we can point out that it is a lazy vowel, so the child will hear people say /ə-lōn/.

It is important to stress all vowel sounds in the spelling lessons. Otherwise, depending on your accent, pen and pin might be indistinguishable.

Also, remember that analyzing words is merely a tool to help us understand spelling. Some words have multiple ways to analyze them. If you see a way to analyze a word that makes more sense to you and your child, use it.

Before We Begin...

There are two kinds of letters, vowels and consonants. The vowels are *a*, *e*, *i*, *o*, and *u*. *Y* is a vowel when it is saying /ĭ/, /ī/, /ē/. When *y* says /y/, it is a consonant. All other letters are also consonants.

Vowels sounds are made when the mouth is open and the sound is not blocked by your tongue, teeth, or lips. Consonant sounds are made when the tongue, teeth, or lips do block the sound.

A syllable is a chunk of a word, and a syllable always has a vowel sound. In fact, when you count the syllables in a word, you are counting how many vowel sounds it has. That's why you can find out how many syllables a word has by seeing how many times your jaw goes down when saying the word—your jaw goes down when you open your mouth to make a vowel sound.

Affixes

Sometimes, we add to a word to make it mean something a little different. It's called a prefix if we add to the beginning of the word, and it's called a suffix if we add to the end of the word. The word without affixes is called the base word.

For instance, someone has a letter. She can **open** it if she wants, or she can leave it **unopened**. She decides she wants to see what the letter says, so now she is **opening** it. The base word is **open**, but we add prefixes and suffixes to make the word mean different things. Yesterday she **opened** it with a letter **opener**, and today she **reopens** it.

When a suffix starts with a vowel, we call it a vowel suffix.

Remember, the base word is the word without prefixes and suffixes. Sometimes the spelling of the base word changes when we add affixes, and some of these changes will be mentioned as you get your new spelling words.

One of the most common suffixes you will encounter is *ed*. You should recognize this as one of your phonograms! When we add it to the end of a word, *ed* tells us that something happened in the past. Sometimes, *ed* will just add a /d/ or /t/ sound to the end of a word. But when the base word ends in the sound /d/ or /t/, *ed* creates a new syllable. In the stories, you will see *ed* added to words you've already learned.

Advanced Phonograms

In the following spelling lists, there are two advanced phonograms.

eau   /ō/, /ū/, /ŏ/ .... bureau, beauty, bureaucracy
sc   /s/ .... scene

spring

sun

shine — *I* says /ī/ because of the silent *e*; underline the silent *e* twice, and draw a bridge between the silent *e* and the *i*.

sun shine — This is a compound word. *I* says /ī/ because of the silent *e*; underline the silent *e* twice, and draw a bridge between the silent *e* and the *i*.

more — *O* says /ō/ because of the silent *e*; underline the silent *e* twice, and draw a bridge between the silent *e* and the *o*.
Alternatively: Mark the phonogram *or*. Double underline the silent *e*. more
$$= 5$$

here — *E* says /ē/ because of the silent *e*; underline the silent *e* twice, and draw a bridge between the silent *e* and the *e*.

glad

food

threw

2
this

su<u>ch</u>

²   ³
b<u>eau</u> ti ful   ***Eau*** is an advanced phonogram which says /ō/, /ū/, /ŏ/—bur<u>eau</u>, b<u>eau</u>ty, bur<u>eau</u>cracy. In levels 1-3, this is the only time it appears. When full is a suffix, it loses an ***l***.

sor r<u>y</u>   [Note: Not the phonogram ***or***. /ŏ-r/.] Underline ***y***. Vowel ***y*** says /ē/ at the end of a multi-syllable word.

²
h<u>air</u>s

nev <u>er</u>

soft

³
pret ti est   Vowel ***y*** changes to ***i*** before adding any ending unless the ending begins with ***i***.

ev <u>er</u>

<u>th</u>ink

hu<u>ng</u>

32

cri<u>ck</u> et	Phonogram **ck** is used only after a single vowel which says its first sound.
plan	
pl<u>a͡c͟e</u>	**A** says /ā/ because of the silent **e**; underline the silent **e** twice, and draw a bridge between the silent **e** and the **a**. **C** says /s/ because of the silent **e**; underline the **c**.
tr<u>y</u>	Underline **y**. Vowel **y** says /ī/ at the end of a one-syllable base word. [Note: This is a spelling rule, so we do not write a number above the vowel. See "Analyzing the Spelling Words" in the the instructions for Part 2.]
buzz	We sometimes double a consonant after a single vowel at the end of a base word.
f<u>ie</u>ld	
fun	

³ ²
to ge<u>th</u> <u>er</u>

²
hid <u>ing</u>   When adding a vowel suffix, we drop the final silent **e** from the base word if it is no longer needed.

squ <u>ea</u>k

sum m<u>er</u>

³   ²
al w<u>ays</u>   When all is a prefix, it loses an *l*.

³
gr<u>ea</u>t

ev <u>er</u> <u>y</u>   Underline *y*. Vowel *y* says /ē/ at the end of a
                     multi-syllable word. [Note: This is an abnormal
                     syllabification of this word to make it easier to
                     sound out.]

<u>wh</u>en

w<u>ai</u>t <u>ing</u>

²
cr<u>ied</u>   Vowel *y* changes to *i* before adding any ending
                     unless the ending begins with *i*.

²
<u>ow</u>n

²   ³
l<u>augh</u> <u>ed</u>

pr<u>ou</u>d

ba by — Underline /ā/; a says /ā/ at the end of a syllable. Underline **y**. Vowel **y** says /ē/ at the end of a multi-syllable word.

stor y — Underline **y**. Vowel **y** says /ē/ at the end of a multi-syllable word. [Note: This is an abnormal syllabification to avoid breaking apart an obvious phonogram.]

dog gie

giv en

our

cun ning

down y — Underline **y**. Vowel **y** says /ē/ at the end of a multi-syllable word.

cry ing — Underline **y**. Vowel **y** says /ī/ at the end of a one-syllable *base* word. **Ing** is a suffix.

bun nies² — Vowel **y** changes to **i** before adding any ending unless the ending begins with **i**.

pic ture — **U** says /ū/ because of the silent **e**; underline the silent **e** twice, and draw a bridge between the silent **e** and the **u**.

lull a by
    3

Underline /ā/; **a** says /ā/ at the end of a syllable. This is not a compound word. Instead, the word "lullaby" is a blend of the words "lull," which means to calm or soothe, and "by," as in good-bye. A lullaby is a song used to sing a baby to sleep.

close
  2

O says /ō/ because of the silent **e**; underline the silent **e** twice, and draw a bridge between the silent **e** and the **o**.

lambs

stars
  2

moon

fall
 3

We often double /l/ after a single vowel at the end of a base word.

sweet

nice

I says /ī/ because of the silent **e**; underline the silent **e** twice, and draw a bridge between the silent **e** and the **i**. **C** says /s/ because of the silent **e**; underline the **c**.

bath

pile

I says /ī/ because of the silent **e**; underline the silent **e** twice, and draw a bridge between the silent **e** and the **i**.

l<u>ea</u>f

bl<u>ew</u>   Definition: for the air to be in motion, past tense.

ca<u>tch</u>   Phonogram **tch** is used only after a single vowel
             which does *not* say its name.

kept

n<u>ea</u>r

bit

saf<u>e</u>   **A** says /ā/ because of the silent **e**; underline the
             silent **e** twice, and draw a bridge between the
             silent **e** and the **a**.

rap

fr<u>ee</u> dom

c**oo**l (with 2 above oo)

sh**a**d**e** (bridge over a-e, double underline e) A says /ā/ because of the silent **e**; underline the silent **e** twice, and draw a bridge between the silent **e** and the **a**.

sw**ing** (underline ing)

thr**ough** (3 above, underline ough)

v**oi** c**e** (=3 under ce) C says /s/ because of the silent **e**; underline the **c**, and double underline the silent **e**.

b**e** l**ow** (2 above ow) Underline /ē/; **e** says /ē/ at the end of a syllable. [Note: This word has a lazy vowel. See "Sounding Out and Lazy Vowels" in the instructions for Part 2.]

r**oo**ts (underline oo)

d**ie** (bridge, double underline e) I says /ī/ because of the silent **e**; underline the silent **e** twice, and draw a bridge between the silent **e** and the **i**.

n**ew** (underline ew)

of f**er** (underline er)

bon͡e̲
O says /ō/ because of the silent *e*; underline the silent *e* twice, and draw a bridge between the silent *e* and the *o*.

a̲ cross
Underline /ā/; *a* says /ā/ at the end of a syllable. We often double /s/ after a single vowel at the end of a base word.

hid͡e̲
I says /ī/ because of the silent *e*; underline the silent *e* twice, and draw a bridge between the silent *e* and the *i*.

bri<u>dge</u>
Phonogram *dge* is used only after a single vowel which says its first sound.

<u>th</u> <u>ou</u>ght

fell
We often double /l/ after a single vowel at the end of a base word.

s<u>ee</u>n

<u>sh</u>a d<u>ow</u>²

grant

cl<u>ai</u>m

kite̲   *I* says /ī/ because of the silent *e*; underline the silent *e* twice, and draw a bridge between the silent *e* and the *i*.

clou̲d̲s²

but te̲r fl̲y   This is a compound word. Underline *y*. Vowel *y* says /ī/ at the end of a one-syllable *base* word.

tie̲   *I* says /ī/ because of the silent *e*; underline the silent *e* twice, and draw a bridge between the silent *e* and the *i*.

stri̲ng̲

o̲ld   Underline /ō/. *O* may say /ō/ when followed by two consonants.

wa̲y̲

slide̲   *I* says /ī/ because of the silent *e*; underline the silent *e* twice, and draw a bridge between the silent *e* and the *i*.

swim

en te̲r

met

fat

f<u>oo</u>l <u>ish</u>

tri<u>ck</u>s   Phonogram **ck** is used only after a single vowel which says its first sound.

bet <u>ter</u>

²
<u>th</u>an

²
n<u>oi</u><u>se</u>₌₅   Double underline the silent **e**.

hunt <u>er</u>

run <u>ning</u>   The base word is one syllable and ends in one vowel followed by one consonant, so we double the final consonant before adding a vowel suffix.

b<u>ar</u>k <u>ing</u>

legs

sh**ort**

2
sl**ow**

3
wa<u>lk</u>   Double underline the silent *l*.

lon**g**

sur**e**   *U* says /ū/ because of the silent *e*; underline the
silent *e* twice, and draw a bridge between the
silent *e* and the *u*.

w<u>or</u>ms

<u>shake</u>   *A* says /ā/ because of the silent *e*; underline the
silent *e* twice, and draw a bridge between the
silent *e* and the *a*.

ha<u>w</u>k

doz en

p<u>ai</u>l

sell — We often double /l/ after a single vowel at the end of a base word. Definition: to exchange something for money.

mon e<u>y</u>²

ha<u>tch</u> <u>ed</u>³ — Phonogram **tch** is used only after a single vowel which does *not* say its name.

c<u>ou</u>nt ed — Phonogram **ed** forms a new syllable when the base word ends in **d** or **t**.

bu <u>y</u> — Underline **y**. Vowel **y** says /ī/ at the end of a one-syllable base word. Definition: to purchase something.

b<u>ui</u>ld

b<u>ui</u>lt

be<u> </u>gan — Underline /ē/; **e** says /ē/ at the end of a syllable.

p<u>oo</u>r

pat ter — The base word is one syllable and ends in one vowel followed by one consonant, so we double the final consonant before adding a vowel suffix.

caught

a fraid — Underline /ā/; *a* says /ā/ at the end of a syllable.

fine — *I* says /ī/ because of the silent *e*; underline the silent *e* twice, and draw a bridge between the silent *e* and the *i*.

hang

bell — We often double /l/ after a single vowel at the end of a base word.

neck — Phonogram *ck* is used only after a single vowel which says its first sound.

joy

wise — *I* says /ī/ because of the silent *e*; underline the silent *e* twice, and draw a bridge between the silent *e* and the *i*.

wis er

hare̲

A says /ā/ because of the silent **e**; underline the silent **e** twice, and draw a bridge between the silent **e** and the **a**.

X
tor toise̲₅

Oi says /ŭ/. Put a small X to show that it's an eXception. Double underline the silent **e**.

hop

3
hopped̲

The base word is one syllable and ends in one vowel followed by one consonant, so we double the final consonant before adding a vowel suffix.

race̲

A says /ā/ because of the silent **e**; underline the silent **e** twice, and draw a bridge between the silent **e** and the **a**. **C** says /s/ because of the silent **e**; underline the **c**.

near ly

Underline **y**. Vowel **y** says /ē/ at the end of a multi-syllable word.

rest

be fore̲

Underline /ē/; **e** says /ē/ at the end of a syllable. **O** says /ō/ because of the silent **e**; underline the silent **e** twice, and draw a bridge between the silent **e** and the **o**.
Alternatively: Mark the phonogram **or**. Double underline the silent **e**. be fore̲ ₅

slept

beats

flapp<u>ed</u> [3] The base word is one syllable and ends in one vowel followed by one consonant, so we double the final consonant before adding a vowel suffix.

call<u>ed</u> [3 2] We often double /l/ after a single vowel at the end of a *base* word. Phonogram **ed** is a suffix.

<u>rea</u> <u>ch</u>

fri<u>e</u>end Memory tip: A fri<u>end</u> is a fri<u>end</u> till the <u>end</u>. If desired, use a colored pencil to underline <u>end</u>. Double underline the silent *i*. This marking emphasizes the memory tip.
Alternatively, **ie** says /ĕ/. Put a small X to show that it's an eXception: fr <u>ie</u> nd

b<u>ea</u>sts

h<u>ur</u>t

<u>kn</u> <u>ew</u>

stay <u>ed</u> [2]

well We often double /l/ after a single vowel at the end of a base word.

hast<u>e</u> **A** says /ā/ because of the silent **e**; underline the silent **e** twice, and draw a bridge between the silent **e** and the **a**.

Thanks giv ing This is a compound word. When adding a
vowel suffix, we drop the final silent *e* from
the base word if it is no longer needed; silent *e*
kept the word from ending in *v*.

in deed

hung ry Underline *y*. Vowel *y* says /ē/ at the end of a
multi-syllable word. [Note: This is an abnormal
syllabification to avoid breaking apart an
obvious phonogram.]

out side This is a compound word. *I* says /ī/ because
of the silent *e*; underline the silent *e* twice, and
draw a bridge between the silent *e* and the *i*.

year

song

loud

wh eat

chil dren

eve ning *E* says /ē/ because of the silent *e*; underline the
silent *e* twice, and draw a bridge between the
silent *e* and the *e*.

noth ing

cones² *O* says /ō/ because of the silent *e*; underline the silent *e* twice, and draw a bridge between the silent *e* and the *o*.

tire *I* says /ī/ because of the silent *e*; underline the silent *e* twice, and draw a bridge between the silent *e* and the *i*.

care *A* says /ā/ because of the silent *e*; underline the silent *e* twice, and draw a bridge between the silent *e* and the *a*.

sh ook²

bright

fair y Underline *y*. Vowel *y* says /ē/ at the end of a multi-syllable word.

asked³

gold Underline /ō/. *O* may say /ō/ when followed by two consonants.

won der³ ful When full is a suffix, it loses an *l*.

stock ing — Phonogram **ck** is used only after a single vowel which says its first sound.

dar ling

cor ner

good ies

ob ject

di rect — Underline /ī/; **i** says /ī/ at the end of a syllable.

sub ject

e vent — Underline /ē/; **e** says /ē/ at the end of a syllable.

in jure — **U** says /ū/ because of the silent **e**; underline the silent **e** twice, and draw a bridge between the silent **e** and the **u**.

in ju ry — Underline /ū/; **u** says /ū/ at the end of a syllable. Underline **y**. Vowel **y** says /ē/ at the end of a multi-syllable word.

49

coun try (4) — Underline **y**. Vowel **y** says /ē/ at the end of a multi-syllable word.

men

sold — Underline /ō/. **O** may say /ō/ when followed by two consonants.

ox en

raise (2) — Double underline the silent **e**.

tax

de lay — Underline /ē/; **e** says /ē/ at the end of a syllable.

de clare — Underline /ē/; **e** says /ē/ at the end of a syllable. **A** says /ā/ because of the silent **e**; underline the silent **e** twice, and draw a bridge between the silent **e** and the **a**.

weigh

firm

flags

hue

Underline /ū/ to show that it's saying /ū/ at the end of a syllable. English words do not end in *u*; underline the silent *e* twice.

stripes

I says /ī/ because of the silent *e*; underline the silent *e* twice, and draw a bridge between the silent *e* and the *i*.

nice

I says /ī/ because of the silent *e*; underline the silent *e* twice, and draw a bridge between the silent *e* and the *i*.

bath

pile

I says /ī/ because of the silent *e*; underline the silent *e* twice, and draw a bridge between the silent *e* and the *i*.

chips

cook

rich

knot

win d<u>ow</u> ²

p<u>ar</u> ad<u>e</u>   *A* says /ā/ because of the silent *e*; underline the
silent *e* twice, and draw a bridge between the
silent *e* and the *a*.

b<u>ir</u> <u>th</u> day   This is a compound word.

str<u>ee</u>t

t<u>o</u>ld   Underline /ō/. *O* may say /ō/ when followed by
two consonants.

tin

dr<u>y</u>   Underline *y*. Vowel *y* says /ī/ at the end of a
one-syllable base word.

<u>sh</u> <u>ar</u>p

st<u>o</u>n<u>e</u>s ²   *O* says /ō/ because of the silent *e*; underline
the silent *e* twice, and draw a bridge between
the silent *e* and the *o*.

<u>a</u> m<u>o</u>ng   Underline /ā/; *a* says /ā/ at the end of a syllable.

gr<u>ai</u>n

plant

² gr<u>ow</u>

rip<u>e</u> *I* says /ī/ because of the silent *e*; underline the silent *e* twice, and draw a bridge between the silent *e* and the *i*.

r<u>ea</u>p

<u>th</u>re<u>sh</u>

fl<u>our</u>

bak<u>e</u> *A* says /ā/ because of the silent *e*; underline the silent *e* twice, and draw a bridge between the silent *e* and the *a*.

l<u>oa</u>f

<u>a</u> g<u>o</u> Underline /ā/; *a* says /ā/ at the end of a syllable.
Underline /ō/; *o* says /ō/ at the end of a syllable.

wh y   Underline **y**. Vowel **y** says /ī/ at the end of a
              one-syllable base word.

bre̲ak³ ing

ha̲rk

ha̲lf   Double underline the silent **l**.

hour   Double underline the silent **h**.

band

set

dew

of ten   The **t** can either be silent or not.

hand

54

grass

We often double /s/ after a single vowel at the end of a base word.

t<u>ur</u> nip

b<u>e</u> c<u>au</u><u>se</u>₅ (²)

Underline /ē/; **e** says /ē/ at the end of a syllable. Double underline the silent **e**.

wolf (X)

O says /ü/. Put a small X to show that it's an eXception. Think to spell /w-ŏ-l-f/.

<u>shin</u> <u>ing</u> (²)

When adding a vowel suffix, we drop the final silent **e** from the base word if it is no longer needed.

sil v<u>er</u>

drink

<u>sh</u>on<u>e</u>

O says /ō/ because of the silent **e**; underline the silent **e** twice, and draw a bridge between the silent **e** and the **o**.

f<u>ee</u>l

ball (³)

We often double /l/ after a single vowel at the end of a base word.

163

s<u>ea</u>   Definition: a body of water.

wīd<u>e</u>   *I* says /ī/ because of the silent *e*; underline the
          silent *e* twice, and draw a bridge between the
          silent *e* and the *i*.

swam

crān<u>e</u>s ²   *A* says /ā/ because of the silent *e*; underline the
          silent *e* twice, and draw a bridge between the
          silent *e* and the *a*.

stro<u>ng</u>

b<u>ea</u>ks

held

cl<u>aw</u>s ²

fat t<u>er</u>   The base word is one syllable and ends in one
          vowel followed by one consonant, so we double
          the final consonant before adding a vowel suffix.

g<u>oe</u>s ²

rob ins

re͟a² son

l͟a͟r͟k

w͟r͟en

can d͟l͟e̳₌₄   Every syllable must have a written vowel; double underline the silent **e**.

quit͟e̳⌢   *I* says /ī/ because of the silent **e**; underline the silent **e** twice, and draw a bridge between the silent **e** and the **i**.

gr͟o͟w²n

past

s͟e͟e͟m

h͟a͟r͟d

b<u>ir</u> d<u>ie</u>

long <u>er</u>

till

We often double /l/ after a single vowel at the end of a base word.

stro<u>ng</u> <u>er</u>

2 2
flies

Vowel *y* changes to *i* before adding any ending unless the ending begins with *i*.

2
rise

I says /ī/ because of the silent *e*; underline the silent *e* twice, and draw a bridge between the silent *e* and the *i*.

2
limbs

sh<u>oo</u>ts

rub b<u>er</u>

Analyze like "one." Think to spell /nōn/, but pronounce /nŭn/. I like this better than treating the word as an exception since /nōn/ and /nŭn/ are close enough to provide a good auditory clue.

Alternatively: Mark as an eXception. *O* says /ŭ/. Put a small X to show that it's an eXception.

Double underline the silent *e*. no^Xne

oak

a̱ cor̲n   Underline /ā/; **a** says /ā/ at the end of a syllable.

trie̱d   Vowel **y** changes to **i** before adding any ending unless the ending begins with **i**.

wo̱ man   Underline /ō/; **o** says /ō/ at the end of a syllable.

clo<u>th</u>

²
bak <u>er</u>

<u>for</u> est

lu<u>ck</u> y̲   Phonogram **ck** is used only after a single vowel which says its first sound. Underline **y**. Vowel **y** says /ē/ at the end of a multi-syllable word.

^x
b<u>ee</u>n   Think to spell /bēn/. Say /běn/.

pa<u>y</u>

pine

I says /ī/ because of the silent *e*; underline the silent *e* twice, and draw a bridge between the silent *e* and the *i*.

nee dles

Every syllable must have a written vowel; double underline the silent *e*.

glass

We often double /s/ after a single vowel at the end of a base word.

broke

O says /ō/ because of the silent *e*; underline the silent *e* twice, and draw a bridge between the silent *e* and the *o*.

hot

hea vy

Underline *y*. Vowel *y* says /ē/ at the end of a multi-syllable word.

rid ing

When adding a vowel suffix, we drop the final silent *e* from the base word if it is no longer needed.

rode

O says /ō/ because of the silent *e*; underline the silent *e* twice, and draw a bridge between the silent *e* and the *o*.

foot

load

2
gos ling

learn

duck ling   Phonogram **ck** is used only after a single vowel which says its first sound.

c<u>o</u>lt   Underline /ō/. **O** may say /ō/ when followed by two consonants.

ca<u>l</u>f   Double underline the silent **l**.

drōv<u>e</u>   **O** says /ō/ because of the silent **e**; underline the silent **e** twice, and draw a bridge between the silent **e** and the **o**. English words do not end in **v**; underline the **v**.

drop

3
ki<u>ck</u> ed   Phonogram **ck** is used only after a single vowel which says its first sound.

dust

3
bu<u>tch</u> er   Phonogram **tch** is used only after a single vowel which does *not* say its name.

gate͇

A says /ā/ because of the silent **e**; underline the silent **e** twice, and draw a bridge between the silent **e** and the **a**.

o͟ pen

Underline /ō/; **o** says /ō/ at the end of a syllable.

wo͟rld

mule͇

U says /ū/ because of the silent **e**; underline the silent **e** twice, and draw a bridge between the silent **e** and the **u**.

³
pull ing

We often double /l/ after a single vowel at the end of a *base* word. **Ing** is a suffix.

²
fri͟ght ene͟d

sh͟ ou͟t ed

Phonogram **ed** forms a new syllable when the base word ends in **d** or **t**.

rid

gri͟nd er͟

Underline /ī/. **I** may say /ī/ when followed by two consonants.

poc͟k et

Phonogram **ck** is used only after a single vowel which says its first sound.

cam el

hump

sn<u>ou</u>t

³
wall

We often double /l/ after a single vowel at the end of a base word.

³
small

We often double /l/ after a single vowel at the end of a base word.

fr<u>ui</u>t

in sīd<u>e</u>

This is a compound word. *I* says /ī/ because of the silent *e*; underline the silent *e* twice, and draw a bridge between the silent *e* and the *i*.

²
ra<u>th</u> er

<u>or</u>

²
<u>thr</u><u>ow</u>

ear ly   Underline **y**. Vowel **y** says /ē/ at the end of a multi-syllable word.

ang ry   Underline **y**. Vowel **y** says /ē/ at the end of a multi-syllable word. [Note: This is an abnormal syllabification to avoid breaking apart an obvious phonogram.]

hair brush   This is a compound word.

comb   Underline /ō/. **O** may say /ō/ when followed by two consonants.

weed

need

grind stone   This is a compound word. Underline /ī/. **I** may say /ī/ when followed by two consonants. **O** says /ō/ because of the silent **e**; underline the silent **e** twice, and draw a bridge between the silent **e** and the **o**.

bank

stooped[3]

watch[3] ed[3]   Phonogram **tch** is used only after a single vowel which does *not* say its name.

<u>wor</u>k

puff   We often double /f/ after a single vowel at the end of a base word.

stand

lil <u>y</u>   Underline **y**. Vowel **y** says /ē/ at the end of a multi-syllable word.

lil <u>ie</u>s²   Vowel **y** changes to **i** before adding any ending unless the ending begins with **i**.

buds

⁵rou<u>gh</u>

brou<u>gh</u>t

gon<u>e</u>₌₅   Double underline the silent **e**.

sun <u>ny</u>   Underline **y**. Vowel **y** says /ē/ at the end of a multi-syllable word.

gruff   We often double /f/ after a single vowel at the end of a base word.

tr<u>o</u>ll   Underline /ō/. **O** may say /ō/ when followed by two consonants. We often double /l/ after a single vowel at the end of a base word.

trap

trip

trip p<u>ing</u>   The base word is one syllable and ends in one vowel followed by one consonant, so we double the final consonant before adding a vowel suffix.

gob ble₌₄   Every syllable must have a written vowel; double underline the silent **e**.

sec ond

big g<u>er</u>   The base word is one syllable and ends in one vowel followed by one consonant, so we double the final consonant before adding a vowel suffix.

2 2
<u>ei</u> <u>th</u> <u>er</u>

an sw<u>er</u> <u>ed</u>²   Double underline the silent **w**.

he<u>ar</u>t   Double underline the silent **e**.

s<u>ee</u>d

bur ied   Vowel **y** changes to **i** before adding any ending
<u>ur</u>   <u>ie</u>   unless the ending begins with **i**.

r<u>ai</u>n drops   This is a compound word.

2
rose

might
<u>igh</u>

2
driv ing   When adding a vowel suffix, we drop the final
<u>ing</u>   silent **e** from the base word if it is no
longer needed; silent **e** kept the word from
ending in **v**.

3
clapp<u>ed</u>   The base word is one syllable and ends in one
vowel followed by one consonant, so we double
the final consonant before adding a vowel suffix.

trade   **A** says /ā/ because of the silent **e**; underline the
silent **e** twice, and draw a bridge between the
silent **e** and the **a**.

l<u>a</u> z<u>y</u>   Underline /ā/; **a** says /ā/ at the end of a syllable.
Underline **y**. Vowel **y** says /ē/ at the end of a
multi-syllable word.

a<u>i</u>r

pl<u>ea</u>s ant

ch <u>i</u>ld   Underline /ī/. *I* may say /ī/ when followed by two consonants.

cat t l<u>e</u>   Every syllable must have a written vowel; double underline the silent *e*.

r<u>oo</u>f

r<u>ei</u>ns

b<u>ee</u>f

w<u>ee</u>k

p<u>or</u>k

don<u>e</u>   Double underline the silent *e*. Think to spell /dŏn/. Say /dŭn/.

kiss

We often double /s/ after a single vowel at the end of a base word.

g<u>o</u>ld en

Underline /ō/. **O** may say /ō/ when followed by two consonants.

f<u>o</u>lks

Underline /ō/. **O** may say /ō/ when followed by two consonants.

<u>ch</u> <u>ee</u>ks

ch<u>a</u>ng<u>e</u>

A says /ā/ because of the silent **e**; underline the silent **e** twice, and draw a bridge between the silent **e** and the **a**. **G** says /j/ because of the silent **e**; underline the **g**.

p<u>ai</u>nt

³   ³
wa<u>sh</u> <u>ed</u>

<u>ar</u>m

l<u>ea</u>st

sak<u>e</u>

A says /ā/ because of the silent **e**; underline the silent **e** twice, and draw a bridge between the silent **e** and the **a**.

sup p<u>er</u>   The base word is "sup," an old word which is not used often now. The base word is one syllable and ends in one vowel followed by one consonant, so we double the final consonant before adding a vowel suffix.

fir<u>e</u>   *I* says /ī/ because of the silent *e*; underline the silent *e* twice, and draw a bridge between the silent *e* and the *i*.

sw<u>ee</u>t

p<u>or</u> ri<u>dge</u>   Phonogram *dge* is used only after a single vowel which says its first sound.

pot

b<u>oi</u>l

stov<u>e</u>   *O* says /ō/ because of the silent *e*; underline the silent *e* twice, and draw a bridge between the silent *e* and the *o*.

fl<u>ow</u> <u>ed</u>   (2 2)

p<u>eo</u> pl<u>e</u>   (with ² ⁴ markings) Think to spell /pē-ō-ple/. Double underline the silent *o*. Underline /ē/; *e* says /ē/ at the end of a syllable. Every syllable must have a written vowel; double underline the silent *e*.

t<u>ur</u>n<u>ed</u>   (2)

cake

A says /ā/ because of the silent **e**; underline the silent **e** twice, and draw a bridge between the silent **e** and the **a**.

spade

A says /ā/ because of the silent **e**; underline the silent **e** twice, and draw a bridge between the silent **e** and the **a**.

r<u>oll</u><u>ed</u>

Underline /ō/. **O** may say /ō/ when followed by two consonants. We often double /l/ after a single vowel at the end of a *base* word. Phonogram **ed** is a suffix.

hav <u>ing</u>

When adding a vowel suffix, we drop the final silent **e** from the base word if it is no longer needed; silent **e** kept the word from ending in **v**.

ly <u>ing</u>

To add the suffix **ing**, drop the final silent **e** from the base word and change the **i** to **y**; English words do not have two letters **i** in a row.

brave

A says /ā/ because of the silent **e**; underline the silent **e** twice, and draw a bridge between the silent **e** and the **a**.

w<u>oo</u>f

d<u>oor</u>

sh <u>ows</u>

h<u>oe</u>

t<u>i</u> n<u>y̱</u>

Underline /ī/; **i** says /ī/ at the end of a syllable. Underline **y**. Vowel **y** says /ē/ at the end of a multi-syllable word.

mu<u>ch</u>

s<u>ou</u> <u>th</u>

<u>e</u>ast

west

⁴
y<u>ou</u> <u>ng</u>

b<u>ur</u>st

sil l<u>y̱</u>

Underline **y**. Vowel **y** says /ē/ at the end of a multi-syllable word.

<u>r</u><u>oo</u>m

⁵
<u>e</u> n<u>ough</u>

Underline /ē/; **e** says /ē/ at the end of a syllable.

dr<u>ea</u>m

gan d<u>er</u>

den

fea th er (2 2)

chim n<u>ey</u> (2)

twin kle<u>=</u>4   Every syllable must have a written vowel; double underline the silent **e**.

blaz <u>ing</u> (2)   When adding a vowel suffix, we drop the final silent **e** from the base word if it is no longer needed.

trav el <u>er</u>

<u>th</u> ough (2 2)

st<u>ar</u>t <u>ed</u>   Phonogram **ed** forms a new syllable when the base word ends in **d** or **t**.

c<u>ur</u>l <u>y</u>
Underline **y**. Vowel **y** says /ē/ at the end of a multi-syllable word.

th <u>or</u>ns²

str<u>aigh</u>t
Double underline the silent **gh**. [Note: **Aigh** is sometimes taught as a phonogram. I choose not to because "straight" is the only common base word in which it appears.]

spin

thr²<u>ea</u>²ds

crab

s<u>ew</u> ˣ
Ew says /ō/ in this word. Put a small X to show that it's an eXception.

st<u>o</u> len
Underline /ō/; **o** says /ō/ at the end of a syllable.

th <u>ie</u>f

s<u>ci</u>s² s<u>or</u>²s²
Sc is an advanced phonogram which says /s/. Alternatively, double underline the silent **c**:
s<u>ci</u>²s s<u>or</u>²s

ja<u>ck</u> al   Phonogram **ck** is used only after a single vowel
which says its first sound.

ten d<u>er</u>

t<u>i</u> g<u>er</u>   Underline /ī/; **i** says /ī/ at the end of a syllable.

prom is<u>ed</u>³

bin

skin

fast <u>er</u>

sh<u>a</u>m<u>e</u>   **A** says /ā/ because of the silent **e**; underline the
silent **e** twice, and draw a bridge between the
silent **e** and the **a**.

<u>a</u>² sh<u>a</u>m<u>ed</u>²   Underline /ā/; **a** says /ā/ at the end of a syllable.

<u>a</u> bl<u>e</u>=4   Underline /ā/; **a** says /ā/ at the end of a syllable.
Every syllable must have a written vowel; double
underline the silent **e**.

2
sh<u>a</u>k ing   When adding a vowel suffix, we drop the
final silent **e** from the base word if it is no
longer needed.

sk<u>y</u>   Underline **y**. Vowel **y** says /ī/ at the end of a
one-syllable base word.

swift l<u>y</u>   Underline **y**. Vowel **y** says /ē/ at the end of a
multi-syllable word.

2
sn<u>ow</u>-flak<u>e̲s</u>   **A** says /ā/ because of the silent **e**; underline the
silent **e** twice, and draw a bridge between the
silent **e** and the **a**.

2
pl<u>ea</u>s ing   When adding a vowel suffix, we drop the
final silent **e** from the base word if it is no
longer needed.

ev <u>er</u> y bod <u>y</u>   This is a compound word. Underline **y**. Vowel
y says /ē/ at the end of a multi-syllable word.

2
tak <u>ing</u>   When adding a vowel suffix, we drop the
final silent **e** from the base word if it is no
longer needed.

2
don k<u>ey</u>

2 3
<u>ea</u>s i <u>er</u>   Vowel **y** changes to **i** before adding any ending
unless the ending begins with **i**.

w<u>o</u> men   Underline /ō/; **o** says /ō/ at the end of a syllable.

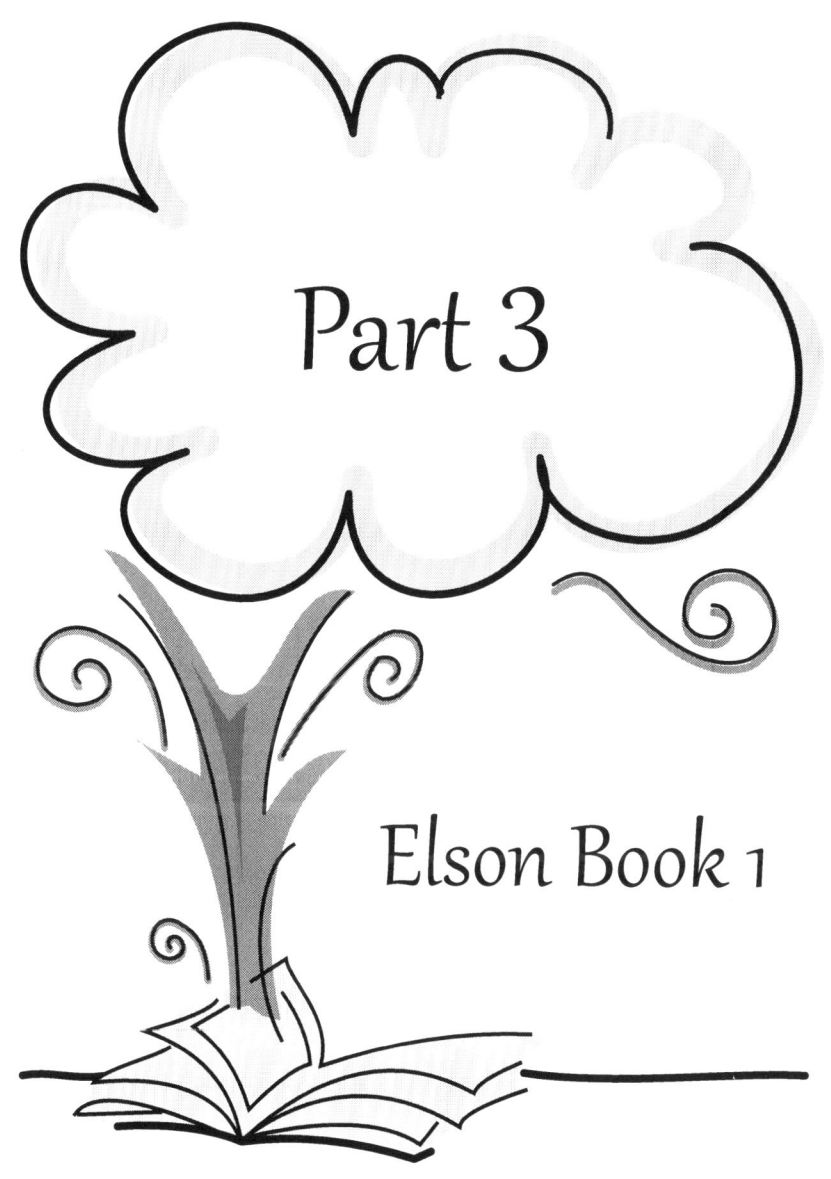

Part 3

Elson Book 1

All the pretty things put by,

Wait upon the children's eye,

Sheep and shepherds, trees and crooks,

In the picture story-books.

Robert Louis Stevenson.

30. Lit-tle Gus-ta-va

Once there was a lit-tle girl.

Her name was Gus-ta-va.

One day she heard a lit-tle bird.

It sang and sang and sang.

"Oh, spring has come!" said Gus-ta-va.

"Moth-er, do you hear the bird?

I am so hap-py! I love the spring."

Her moth-er gave her some bread
and milk.

She sat in the warm sun to eat it.

Lit-tle Gray Kit-ten saw her there.

She ran to Gus-ta-va.

"Mew, mew," said the kit-ten.

"What have you to eat?"

"I have bread and milk," said Gus-ta-va.

"Will you have some?

I will give you some of my good milk."

"Mew, mew," said Gray Kit-ten.

"It is good. Give me some more."

"Oh, I am so hap-py," said Gus-ta-va.

"Spring is here, Gray Kit-ten."

"I like spring, too," said Gray Kit-ten.

Soon lit-tle Brown Hen came by.

"Good day, Brown Hen," said Gus-ta-va.

"I am glad to see you.

Here is some bread for you.

Eat all you want.

Spring is here, Brown Hen.

Are you not glad?

I am so glad that win-ter is o-ver.

Do take some more bread."

"Cluck, cluck," said lit-tle Brown Hen.

"Spring makes me hap-py, too."

"Coo, coo; coo, coo," said the doves.

"Oh, I hear my white doves,"

said Gus-ta-va.

They flew down to her.

"I am so glad to see you," she said.

"How pret-ty your white wings are!

Win-ter is o-ver, White Doves.

Now you can find food.

But I will give you some bread to-day."

She threw them some bread.

"Oh, spring has come," said Gus-ta-va.

"We are all so hap-py."

"We like spring, too," said the doves.

Soon her lit-tle dog came by.

"Bow-wow, bow-wow," he said.

"Don't you want me, too?"

"Oh, yes, Lit-tle Dog," said Gus-ta-va.

"You must have some food, too.

Spring is here, Lit-tle Dog.

We are so glad that win-ter is o-ver.

Take some of this milk.

I have not had an-y yet.

But take all you want.

I will put it on the floor for you.

I like to see you eat."

Then Gus-ta-va sat down on the floor.

Lit-tle Dog, Gray Kit-ten, Brown Hen, and the White Doves sat a-round her.

Just then her moth-er came out.

"Oh, Gus-ta-va!" she said. "You have no din-ner.

I will get you some more bread and milk."

"I gave it all a-way," said Gus-ta-va.

"Spring made me so hap-py."

Adapted from the Poem by Celia Thaxter.

31. Who Took the Bird's Nest?

"Tweet-tweet, tweet-tweet!" said
Yel-low Bird.

"I made a pret-ty lit-tle nest.

I made it in the lit-tle tree.

I put four eggs in it.

Then I flew to the brook.

How hap-py I was!

But now I can-not find my nest.

What shall I do? What shall I do?

I will see if White Cow took it."

"Tweet-tweet, tweet-tweet!" said
Yel-low Bird.

"White Cow, did you take a-way
my nest?"

"Oh, no!" said "White Cow. "Not I!

I did not take a-way your nest.

I would not do such a thing.

I gave you some hay for your nest.

I saw you put your nest in the lit-tle tree.

You sang and sang and sang.

It was a beau-ti-ful lit-tle nest.

I am sor-ry you can-not find it.

But I did not take it," said White Cow.

"Oh, no! I would not do such a thing."

"Tweet-tweet, tweet-tweet!" said
Yel-low Bird.

"Who took my lit-tle nest?

Oh! Here comes Brown Dog.

Brown Dog, did you take a-way my nest?

I put it in the lit-tle tree.

There were four eggs in it."

"Oh, no!" said Brown Dog. "Not I!

I would not do such a thing.

I gave you some hairs for your nest.

I am sor-ry you can-not find it.

But I did not take it. Oh, no!

I would nev-er do such a thing!"

"Tweet-tweet, tweet-tweet!" said
Yel-low Bird.

"Who took my lit-tle nest?

Oh! Here comes Black Sheep.

Black Sheep, did you take a-way my nest?

I put it in the lit-tle tree.

Then I flew to the brook."

"Oh, no!" said Black Sheep. "Not I.

I would nev-er do such a thing.

I gave you wool to make your nest soft.

It was the pret-ti-est nest I ev-er saw.

Oh, no! I did not take it a-way.

I would nev-er do such a thing."

"Moo, moo!" said White Cow.

"Bow-wow!" said Brown Dog.

"Baa, baa!" said Black Sheep.

"Who took Yel-low Bird's nest?

We think a lit-tle boy took it.

We wish we could find him."

A lit-tle boy heard them.

He hung his head.

Then he ran in-to the house and hid

be-hind the bed.

He would not eat his din-ner.

Can you guess why?

The lit-tle boy felt ver-y sor-ry.

Soon he came out of the house a-gain.

He took the nest back to the lit-tle tree.

"Dear Yel-low Bird," he said, "I

am sor-ry.

I took your nest from the lit-tle tree.

But I will nev-er do such a thing a-gain."

"Tweet-tweet, tweet-tweet, tweet-

tweet!" sang Yel-low Bird.

"I am as hap-py as can be."

Adapted from the Poem by Lydia Maria Child.

32. The Mouse, the Crick-et, and the Bee

Once there was a lit-tle mouse.

One spring day she sat in the sun.

A crick-et and a bee came a-long.

"Win-ter is o-ver," said the lit-tle mouse.

"Let us make a house.

We are so lit-tle.

We can all live in one lit-tle house.

We can be so hap-py there."

"That is a good plan," said the crick-et.

"I like that plan, too," said the bee.

"Where shall we make a house?" said the bee.

"Let us find a ver-y dark place," said the crick-et.

"I like the dark.

It is dark un-der the barn.

The sun can-not find us there.

I like to chirp in the dark.

I do not like the light."

"Oh, dear! Oh, dear!" said the mouse.

"I do not like to live in the dark.

I am not hap-py in the dark.

The warm sun is the place for me.

Let us try to find a light place."

"Yes, yes!" said the bee. "Yes, yes!

I like the sun-shine, too.

I know a good place for a house.

It is up in a tall tree.

It is ver-y light there.

The tree is in a pret-ty mead-ow.

The mead-ow has flow-ers in it.

The sun will keep us warm.

The wind will sing to us.

I like to buzz in the sun-shine.

I am ver-y hap-py in the sun-shine."

"Oh, dear! Oh, dear!" said the crick-et.

"I nev-er chirp in the sun-shine, and I can-not fly.

I can-not live in a tall tree.

Oh, dear, no! That place would not do for me.

What shall I do? What shall I do?"

"Let us try my place," said the mouse.

"I know a good place for a house.

It is on the ground.

It is in the sun-shine, too.

I like to live in a corn field.

We can eat the corn.

We can run and play in the sun-shine.

That will be such fun.

I can make a warm home for us.

There we can be ver-y hap-py."

"Oh, dear! Oh, dear!" said the bee.

"I can-not eat corn.

That place would not do for me.

We can-not live to-geth-er."

So the bee flew to the tall tree.

"Buzz, buzz," she sang in the sun-shine.

"See how high I am.

My home is best."

The crick-et ran un-der the barn.

"Chirp, chirp," he sang in the dark.

"I have a good hid-ing place.

My home is best."

The mouse ran in-to the field.

She made a soft, warm nest.

"Squeak, squeak," she said in the corn.

"My home is best."

She went to sleep in the sun-shine.

Adapted from the Poem by Sidney Dayre.

33. Bob-bie's Yel-low Chick-en

Bob-bie's grand-moth-er lived on a farm.

One sum-mer he went to see her.

He saw man-y cows and sheep there.

He saw man-y hors-es and pigs, too.

Bob-bie lived on the farm all sum-mer.

He was as hap-py as he could be.

One day he said, "Grand-moth-er, I
wish I could live here al-ways.

I have great fun here."

One day Grand-moth-er went to the barn.

Bob-bie went with her.

She said, "See this lit-tle yel-low chick-en, Bob-bie."

"May I have her?" said Bob-bie.

"She is the pret-ti-est chick-en I ev-er saw."

"Yes, Bob-bie," said Grand-moth-er.

"You may have her.

You must give her food ev-er-y day.

Some day she will lay an egg for you."

Bob-bie gave her food all sum-mer.

She grew and grew and grew.

One day Grand-moth-er said, "Bob-bie, your moth-er wants you to come home.

You may come a-gain next sum-mer."

Bob-bie felt sor-ry to leave the farm.

He went to the barn.

"Good-bye, lit-tle yel-low chick-en," he said.

"I must go home to moth-er.

Please do not for-get me.

I will see you a-gain next sum-mer."

"I will not for-get you, Bob-bie," said the lit-tle yel-low chick-en.

"When you come back I will lay an egg for you."

Bob-bie went home to his moth-er.

His moth-er was wait-ing for him.

How glad she was to see him!

Bob-bie was glad to see her, too.

"Oh, Moth-er!" he cried, "Grand-moth-er gave me a lit-tle yel-low chick-en.

I gave it food and wa-ter ev-er-y day.

It is my own lit-tle chick-en.

Next sum-mer it will lay big white eggs for me.

Do you think it will know me when I go back?"

The next sum-mer Bob-bie went back to Grand-moth-er's.

He ran at once to the barn.

He looked and looked and looked, but he could not see his lit-tle chick-en.

Just then he saw a big brown hen jump off her nest.

Grand-moth-er laughed. "There is your lit-tle yel-low chick-en," she said.

"You did not know her when you saw her."

"Oh, see the egg in her nest!" said Bob-bie.

"I did not know my lit-tle yel-low chick-en.

But she did not for-get to lay an egg for me."

How proud the big brown hen was!

Carolyn S. Bailey, Adapted.

34. The Go-to-Sleep Stor-y

"I must go to bed," said lit-tle dog Pen-ny.

"But first I must say good night to Ba-by Ray.

He is kind to me.

He gives me some of his bread and milk.

I will see if he is a-sleep."

So lit-tle dog Pen-ny found Ba-by Ray.

His moth-er was tell-ing him a Go-to-Sleep stor-y.

Lit-tle dog Pen-ny heard it.

This is what he heard:

> The dog-gie that was giv-en him to
> keep, keep, keep.
> Went to see if Ba-by Ray was
> a-sleep, sleep, sleep.

"We must go to bed, too," said the
two kit-tens.

"But first we must say good night to
Ba-by Ray.

He gives us milk for our din-ner.

Let us see if he is a-sleep."

So the lit-tle kit-tens found Ba-by Ray.

They heard the Go-to-Sleep stor-y.

This is what they heard:

> One dog-gie that was giv-en him to
> keep, keep, keep.

Two cun-ning lit-tle kit-ty cats,

creep, creep, creep,

Went to see if Ba-by Ray was

a-sleep, sleep, sleep.

"We must go to bed, too," said the
three bun-nies.

"But first we must say good night to
Ba-by Ray.

He gives us green leaves for our din-ner.

Let us see if he is a-sleep."

So the bun-nies found Ba-by Ray.

They heard the Go-to-Sleep stor-y.

This is what they heard:

One dog-gie that was giv-en him to

keep, keep, keep,

Two cun-ning lit-tle kit-ty cats,

creep, creep, creep.

Three pret-ty lit-tle bun-nies with a
leap, leap, leap,
Went to see if Ba-by Ray was
a-sleep, sleep, sleep.

"We must go to bed," said the four
white geese.

"But first we must say good night to
Ba-by Ray. He gives us corn.

Let us see if he is a-sleep."

So the four geese found Ba-by Ray.

They heard the Go-to-Sleep stor-y.

This is what they heard:

One dog-gie that was giv-en him to
keep, keep, keep.

Two cun-ning lit-tle kit-ty cats,
creep, creep, creep,

Three pret-ty lit-tle bun-nies with a
leap, leap, leap,

Four geese from a duck pond, deep,
deep, deep.
Went to see if Ba-by Ray was
a-sleep, sleep, sleep.

"We must go to bed," said the five
lit-tle chicks.
"But first we must say good night to
Ba-by Ray.
He gives us bread.
Let us see if he is a-sleep."
So the five lit-tle chicks found Ba-by Ray.
He was just go-ing to sleep.

They heard all of the Go-to-Sleep stor-y.
This is what they heard:

One dog-gie that was giv-en him to
keep, keep, keep,
Two cun-ning lit-tle kit-ty cats,
creep, creep, creep.
Three pret-ty lit-tle bun-nies, with a
leap, leap, leap,
Four geese from the duck pond,
deep, deep, deep.
Five down-y lit-tle chicks, cry-ing
peep, peep, peep.
All saw that Ba-by Ray was a-sleep,
sleep, sleep.

Eudora Bumstead, Adapted.

35. A Lull-a-by

Lull-a-by, oh, lull-a-by!

Flow-ers are closed and lambs are sleep-ing;

Lull-a-by, oh, lull-a-by!

Stars are up; the moon is peep-ing;

Lull-a-by, oh, lull-a-by!

Sleep, my ba-by, fall a-sleep-ing,

Lull-a-by, oh, lull-a-by!

Christina G. Rossetti.

36. The Ant and the Dove

"I want some wa-ter," an ant once said.

"I will go to the brook.

I can get some wa-ter there."

So she went to the brook.

But she tum-bled in-to the wa-ter.

"Help! Help!" she cried.

"The wa-ter is cold!"

A dove heard the ant.

"I will help you!" cried the dove.

So she threw a leaf in-to the brook.

The ant got on the leaf.

"Ooo-oo-o-o!" blew the wind.

It blew the leaf to the land.

Then the ant got off the leaf.

"Thank you, kind dove," she said.

"Some-time I will help you."

Soon a man came by.

He saw the pret-ty dove.

He said, "I will catch her."

So he kept ver-y still.

He came ver-y near to the dove.

"Coo, coo!" said the pret-ty dove.

She did not see the man.

But the ant saw him.

She said, "I will help the good dove."

So she bit the man and made him jump.

The man cried out, "Oh! Oh!"

Then the dove saw the man.

A-way she flew!

She was safe, and the ant was hap-py.

Retold from a Fable by Aesop.

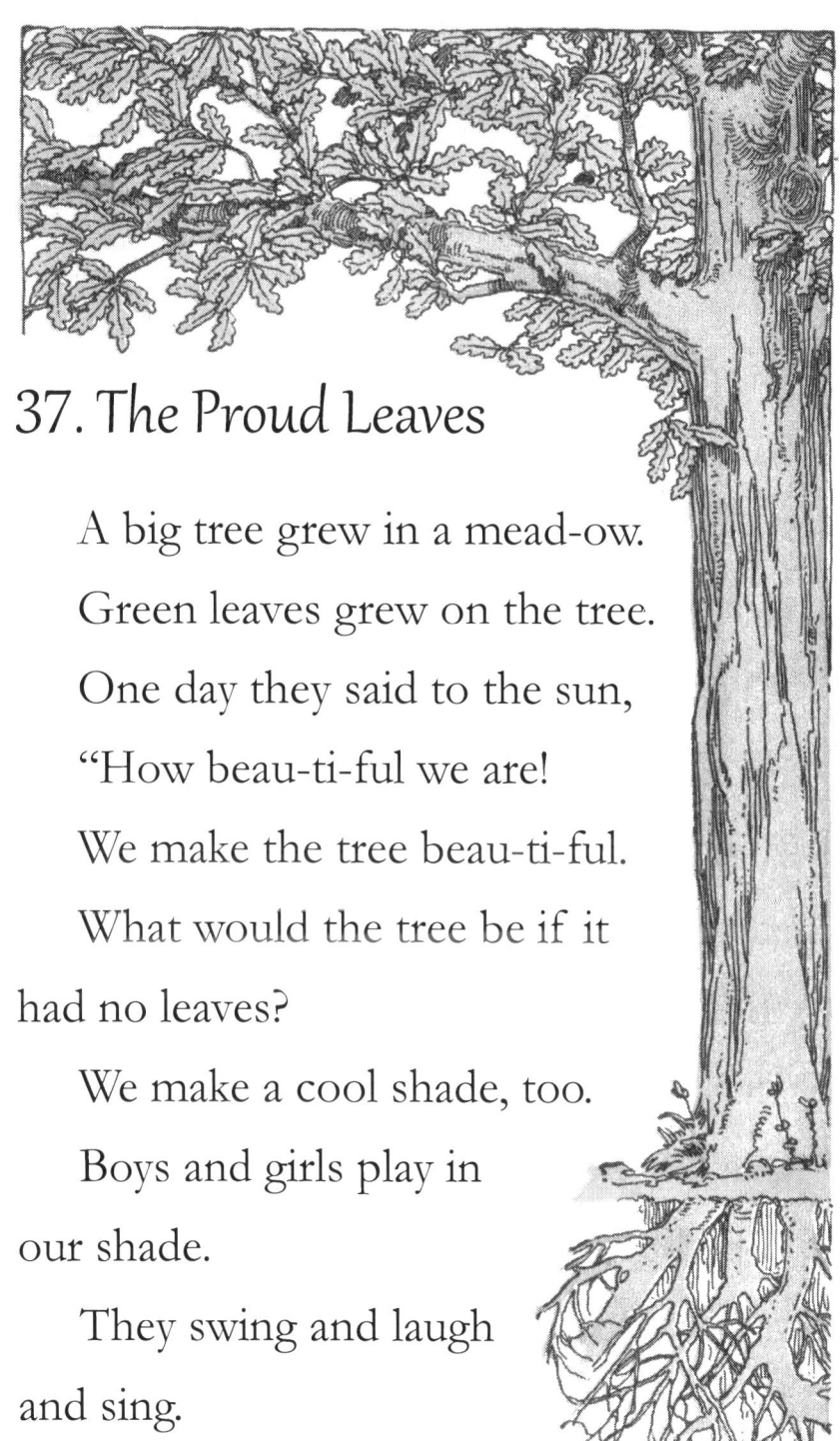

37. The Proud Leaves

A big tree grew in a mead-ow.

Green leaves grew on the tree.

One day they said to the sun,

"How beau-ti-ful we are!

We make the tree beau-ti-ful.

What would the tree be if it

had no leaves?

We make a cool shade, too.

Boys and girls play in

our shade.

They swing and laugh

and sing.

All the birds fly in-to the tree.

They sing to us,

'Tweet-tweet, tweet-tweet.'

See their lit-tle nests all a-round us!

The wind sings through us.

It says, "Oo-oo-o-o! Oo-oo-o-o!
Oo-oo-o-o!"

So the leaves felt ver-y proud.

All at once they heard a soft lit-tle
voice far be-low. It said, "Leaves, we
help the tree, too."

"Who are you?" said the leaves.

"We are the roots," said the voice. "We
get food for you.

You are beau-ti-ful, but you die.

New leaves come ev-er-y spring.

But we live on and on.

If we should die, the great tree would die, too."

The leaves said, "You do help the tree, kind roots.

We will not for-get you a-gain."

A Russian Fable.

38. The Dog and His Shad-ow

Once there was a big dog.

When he got a bone he al-ways hid it.

He nev-er gave a bit to an-y oth-er dog.

If he saw a lit-tle dog with a bone he
would say,

"Bow-wow! Give me that bone!"

Then he would take the bone.

One day he took a bone from a lit-tle dog.

"The lit-tle dog shall not find this
bone," he said. "I will take it far a-way.

I will go a-cross the brook and hide it."

So the big dog ran to the brook.

There was a lit-tle bridge o-ver the brook.

The dog ran out on the bridge.

He looked down in-to the wa-ter and thought he saw an-oth-er dog there.

He thought the dog had a bone, too.

"I will take that bone," said the big dog.

"Then I shall have two bones. Bow-wow! Bow-wow!" said the big dog.

Then his own bone fell out of his mouth.

It fell in-to the brook.

The big dog could not get it out.

There was no dog in the wa-ter at all!

The big dog had seen his own shad-ow.

Retold from a Fable by Aesop.

39. The Kite and the But-ter-fly

A kite flew far up in-to the clouds.

It played with the wind.

It looked at the sun.

The kite saw a but-ter-fly
far be-low.

"Look at me!" said the kite.

"See how high I am!

I can see far, far a-way.

Maybe I shall fly to the sun.

Don't you wish you were a kite?

Then you could fly with me."

"Oh, no!" said the but-ter-fly.

"I do not fly ver-y high.

But I go where I please.

You fly ver-y high.

But you are tied to a string!"

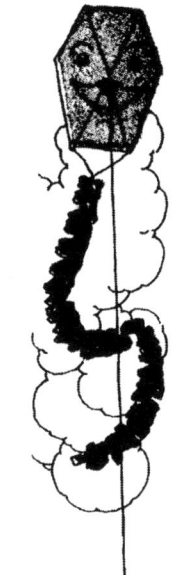

A Russian Fable.

40. The Cat and the Fox

One day a cat met a fox in the woods.

They were looking for food.

The cat want-ed a fat mouse.

The fox want-ed a fat rab-bit.

They had looked and looked.

But all the fat rab-bits and
all the fat mice were hid-ing.

The fox was ver-y cross.

When he want-ed a rab-bit,
he want-ed it!

The cat was not cross at all.

When she want-ed a mouse,
she could wait for it.

She said, "Good morn-ing,
Mr. Fox.

I am glad to see you.

How are you get-ting on?"

The fox looked at the cat and laughed.

"You fool-ish lit-tle cat!" he said.

"I can al-ways get a-long all right.

I know so man-y tricks.

How man-y tricks do you know?"

"I know just one trick," said the cat.

"Ha, ha!" laughed the fox.

"Just one lit-tle trick! What is that?"

"I can jump up in-to a tree," said the cat.

"When the dogs come—jump! I am safe!"

"Ha, ha!" laughed the fox.

"Just one lit-tle trick!

I know man-y tricks. They are all bet-ter than your trick, too.

Let me tell you some of them.

Then the dogs will nev-er catch you."

"All right!" said the cat.

Just then they heard a great noise.

It was a hunt-er on his horse.

His dogs were run-ning and bark-ing.

Jump! The cat was safe in a tree!

But the dogs got Mr. Fox!

"I am just a fool-ish lit-tle cat," said the cat.

"I know only one trick.

But one trick is some-times bet-ter than man-y."

Retold from a Fable by Aesop.

41. A Wish

May: Oh, see the
      pret-ty birds!
      How fast
      they fly!
      They look
      so hap-py.
      I wish I had wings.
      Then I could fly, too.
      But I have only legs.
      My legs are short, and
      they are slow, too.
      Wings can go fast.
      When I go home I must walk.
      It will take me a long time.
      I must go through the mead-ow.
      Then there is such a hill to go up!
      I do not like to go up high hills.

Oh, if I were on-ly a bird!

How fast I would fly home

to moth-er!

Bird: Are you sure you would like to

be a bird?

I eat worms for my din-ner.

May: Oh, dear! I did not think of that!

I should not like to eat worms.

I like bread and milk for my din-ner.

Bird: Would you like to sleep up in a tree?

My lit-tle ones like a tree-top bed.

May: Oh, no! That would not do at all!

The wind some-times shakes the tree.

It would shake me out of the nest.

My lit-tle white bed is best for me.

Bird: What would you do when
the hawk came? My lit-tle birds hide
from the hawk.

May: I am so big the hawk would see me.
Oh, I am so glad I am not a bird!
It is best for me to be a girl.

42. Mol-ly and the Pail of Milk

Mol-ly lived on a farm.

A lit-tle cow lived on the farm, too.

The cow gave good milk.

One day Mol-ly's moth-er said, "You may have this pail of milk, Mol-ly.

Go to town and sell it.

You may have all the mon-ey you get."

"Oh, thank you, Moth-er!" said Mol-ly.

She put the pail of milk on her head and walked down the road.

"When I sell this milk, I shall get some mon-ey," she said.

"Then I will buy some eggs.

I will put the eggs un-der our hens.

The hens will sit on the eggs.

Soon lit-tle chick-ens will be hatched.

I will sell the chick-ens.

With the mon-ey I will buy more eggs.

I will buy man-y, man-y eggs.

Soon I shall have man-y lit-tle chick-ens.

They will grow big and fat.

I will sell them all.

What shall I do with all that mon-ey?

Oh, I know! I will buy some geese.

Then I will buy some ducks.

I will buy a pig.

I will buy a horse.

I will buy a cow.

I will buy a farm.

I will build a lit-tle house on the farm.

I will live in the lit-tle house.

How hap-py I shall be there!

This lit-tle pail of milk will do it all."

It made Mol-ly hap-py just to think of it.

She be-gan to jump and sing.

Down came the pail of milk!

Poor Mol-ly! She did not sell the milk.

She could not buy an-y eggs.

She could not buy ducks and geese, a pig, a horse, a cow, and a lit-tle farm.

She could not build a lit-tle house.

She count-ed her chick-ens too soon.

Next time she will wait un-til they are hatched.

Retold from a Fable by Aesop.

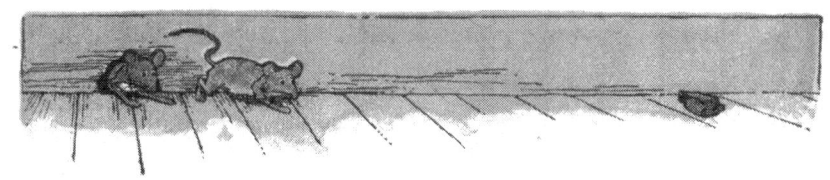

43. The Fine Plan

Once some mice lived in a big house.

They ran all o-ver the house.

Pat-ter, pat-ter, pat-ter, went their feet!

The house was full of mice.

A cat lived in the big house, too.

He was a big cat.

He liked to catch the mice.

He caught some ev-er-y day.

The mice were a-fraid of him.

They said, "What shall we do?

This big cat will catch us all.

He will eat us up.

Oh, what shall we do?"

"I know what to do," said a lit-tle mouse.

"The cat makes no noise when he walks.

We can-not hear him.

I have a fine plan.

We must hang a bell on his neck.

The bell will make a noise.

Ting-a-ling! Ting-a-ling! it will go.

We shall hear the bell. Then we shall know that the cat is com-ing.

We will run a-way.

The cat can-not catch us."

"What a fine plan!" said the oth-er mice.

"Yes! Yes! The cat must have a bell on his neck!

Then he can-not catch us."

The mice jumped for joy.

The lit-tle mouse was ver-y proud.

"How wise I am!" he said.

"Now we shall be safe."

But Old Gray Mouse laughed.

He was wis-er than the lit-tle mouse.

"Ha, ha!" he laughed, "Ha, ha, ha!

That is a fine plan, lit-tle mouse.

But who will hang the bell on the cat?

Will you, lit-tle mouse?"

"Oh, no, no! He would eat me up!"

But some-one must put the bell on the cat!

The lit-tle mouse had not thought of that.

He ran a-way as fast as he could go.

He cried "Squeak! Squeak!" all the way home.

Retold from a Fable by Aesop.

44. The Race

One day a lit-tle
hare was in a mead-ow.

A lit-tle tor-toise was
there, too.

He was creep-ing to the
riv-er for a swim.

"How slow you are!" said the hare.

"You can-not hop. You can only creep.

Look at me! See how fast I hop!"

And the lit-tle hare gave a great hop.

"I am slow," said the tor-toise.

"But I am sure.

Would you like to run a race with me?"

"Run a race!" cried the hare.

"How fool-ish that would be!

I hop and you creep.

How can we run a race?"

"Let us try," said the tor-toise.

"Let us race to the riv-er.

We shall see who gets there first."

"The riv-er is a long way off," said the hare.

"But I shall soon be there. Good-bye!"

Off went the lit-tle hare, hop, hop, hop!

Off went the tor-toise, creep, creep, creep.

Soon the hare was near-ly to the riv-er.

It was a warm day.

"I will rest a lit-tle," he said.

So the hare rest-ed and ate some leaves.

Then he felt sleep-y.

"It is ver-y warm," he said.

"I will sleep a lit-tle.

That fool-ish old tor-toise is slow.

I shall wake up be-fore he creeps here.

Then I can hop to the riv-er.

I shall be there long be-fore he comes."

So the lit-tle hare went to sleep.

The lit-tle tor-toise came creep-ing on.

He did not stop to eat.

He did not stop to sleep.

He went on and on, creep, creep, creep.

By and by he came to the riv-er.

The lit-tle hare slept a long time.

Then he woke up with a jump.

"Dear me! I must hop a-long," he said.

"Where can that slow tor-toise be?

He is not here yet."

The lit-tle hare hopped on to the riv-er.

There was the lit-tle tor-toise wait-ing for him!

"Creep and creep

Beats hop and sleep!"

said the tor-toise.

Retold from a Fable by Aesop.

45. The Roos-ter and the Fox

One morn-ing a roos-ter flew to the top of the barn.

He flapped his wings and called, "Cock-a-doo-dle-doo!"

Now a fox heard the roos-ter.

So he came to the barn.

He want-ed to get the roos-ter and eat him.

But the fox could not reach him.

So he called up to the roos-ter, "Come down, friend!

Have you heard the news?

The beasts and the birds are go-ing to live to-geth-er.

They will not hurt each oth-er an-y-more.

They will not eat each oth-er up.

They will all be friends.

Come down, friend roos-ter!

Let us talk a-bout the news."

But the roos-ter knew the fox had man-y tricks.

So he stayed on top of the barn.

He looked far, far a-way.

"What do I see? What do I see?" said he.

"Well, what do you see?" asked the fox.

The roos-ter looked far, far a-way.

"Oh! The dogs are com-ing! The dogs are com-ing!" he said.

The fox got up in great haste.

"Good-bye," he said. "I must go!"

"Oh, no, friend," said the roos-ter. "Don't go.

The dogs won't hurt you, will they?

You said the beasts and the birds were go-ing to live to-geth-er and be friends.

Let us talk a-bout the great news."

"No, no! I must run a-way," said the fox.

"Maybe the dogs have not heard the news."

So he ran off as fast as he could go.

That time the roos-ter was wis-er than the fox.

Retold from a Fable by Aesop.

Story 46 Pre-Lesson

In this poem, a rooster cheers. There's an advanced phonogram which you have not learned in the second syllable. It says /ä/ like the third sound of *a*. Can you sound it out?

hur-rah

46. Thanks-giv-ing in the Hen House

Brown Hen: This is Thanks-giv-ing Day.

How cold it is!

It has snowed all day.

Gray Goose: Indeed it has.

I do not like this day at all.

I wish Jack would come.

It is time for our din-ner.

Maybe he will for-get us to-day.

Lit-tle Chick: Peep, peep! I am hun-gry,
     too. All the lit-tle chicks are hun-gry.

Red Roos-ter: Cheer up, Brown Hen.
     Cheer up, Gray Goose.
     Cheer up, Lit-tle Chick.
     This is Thanks-giv-ing Day.
     We must all be hap-py to-day.

Brown Hen: We can-not be hap-py, Red
     Roos-ter, when we are hun-gry.
     We want some wa-ter, too.
     We don't like to eat snow.

Gray Goose: How cold it is out-side!

Red Roos-ter: But it is warm in here.
     Jack has filled all the cracks
     to keep us warm.

The wind can-not hurt us now.

And the fox can-not get us.

I am hun-gry, too, but I won't

be sad to-day.

This is the best day of the year.

Big Tur-key: Red Roos-ter, you are right.

Brown Hen and Gray Goose are

too cross.

We should all be hap-py to-day.

Red Roos-ter: Let us sing a glad

Thanks-giv-ing song.

Will you sing first, Brown Hen?

You have a fine voice.

Brown Hen: Cut—cut—ca—da—cut!

Red Roos-ter: Now let us all

sing to-geth-er.

Sing loud. There! That is fine.

Moth-er: What a noise in the hen house!

The poor chick-ens want their

Thanks-giv-ing din-ner.

Fa-ther: Jack, you for-got them!

Take them some food.

Jack: Yes, indeed I will.

I will give them a basket of

corn and wheat.

Hol-ly: And I will take them some wa-ter.

Poor chick-ens! They have not had

an-y Thanks-giv-ing din-ner.

Let us run to the hen house.

Gray Goose: Here come Jack and Mol-ly.

   Jack has a basket of corn and wheat.

Brown Hen: And Mol-ly is bring-ing a

   pail of wa-ter, too.

Red Roos-ter: Hur-rah! I guess the chil-

   dren liked our Thanks-giv-ing song.

   Let us all sing a-gain.

   One, two, three, sing!

Jack: How hap-py they all are in the

   hen house this eve-ning!

Hol-ly: They like Thanks-giv-ing Day, too.

Frances M. Fox.

47. The Christ-mas Fair-y

It was the day be-fore Christ-mas.

Two lit-tle chil-dren went to the woods.

They want-ed to find a Christ-mas tree.

Poor lit-tle chil-dren! They had nev-er had a Christ-mas tree.

"Oh, dear!" said the lit-tle girl.

"We have noth-ing to put on the tree."

"We must find a tree with man-y cones on it," said the lit-tle boy.

"Cones will make our tree beau-ti-ful."

"Yes, yes!" said the lit-tle girl.

"We must find a tree with cones on it."

The chil-dren walked on and on.

But they could not find a tree with cones on it.

By and by night came.

The chil-dren were ver-y, ver-y tired.

They could not find their way home.

So they sat down to rest.

Soon the lit-tle girl fell a-sleep.

The lit-tle boy was tired, too, but he did not close his eyes.

"I must take care of sis-ter," he said.

"I will put my coat a-round her to keep her warm."

He sat there a long time un-til he shook with the cold.

By and by he saw a ver-y bright light.

It woke his lit-tle sis-ter.

Soon the chil-dren saw a beau-ti-ful fair-y.

She came right up to them.

"Who are you?" asked the lit-tle boy.

"I am the Christ-mas Fair-y," said the fair-y.

"I am al-ways in the woods at Christ-mas time.

I make the woods bright at night.

Then good lit-tle boys and girls can find the pret-ti-est trees.

Come, chil-dren! I will take you to a beau-ti-ful tree."

The fair-y took them to a beau-ti-ful tree.

It had man-y, man-y cones on it.

"Here is your tree," said the fair-y.

Then she said, "Lit-tle cones, light the tree."

The lit-tle cones be-gan to shine like gold.

"Oh, what a won-der-ful Christ-mas tree!" said the chil-dren.

"It will light you all the way home," said the fair-y.

"It will shine for you on Christ-mas Day, too."

The chil-dren took the beau-ti-ful tree.

It light-ed them all the way home.

They were ver-y, ver-y hap-py.

Edna V. Riddleberger.

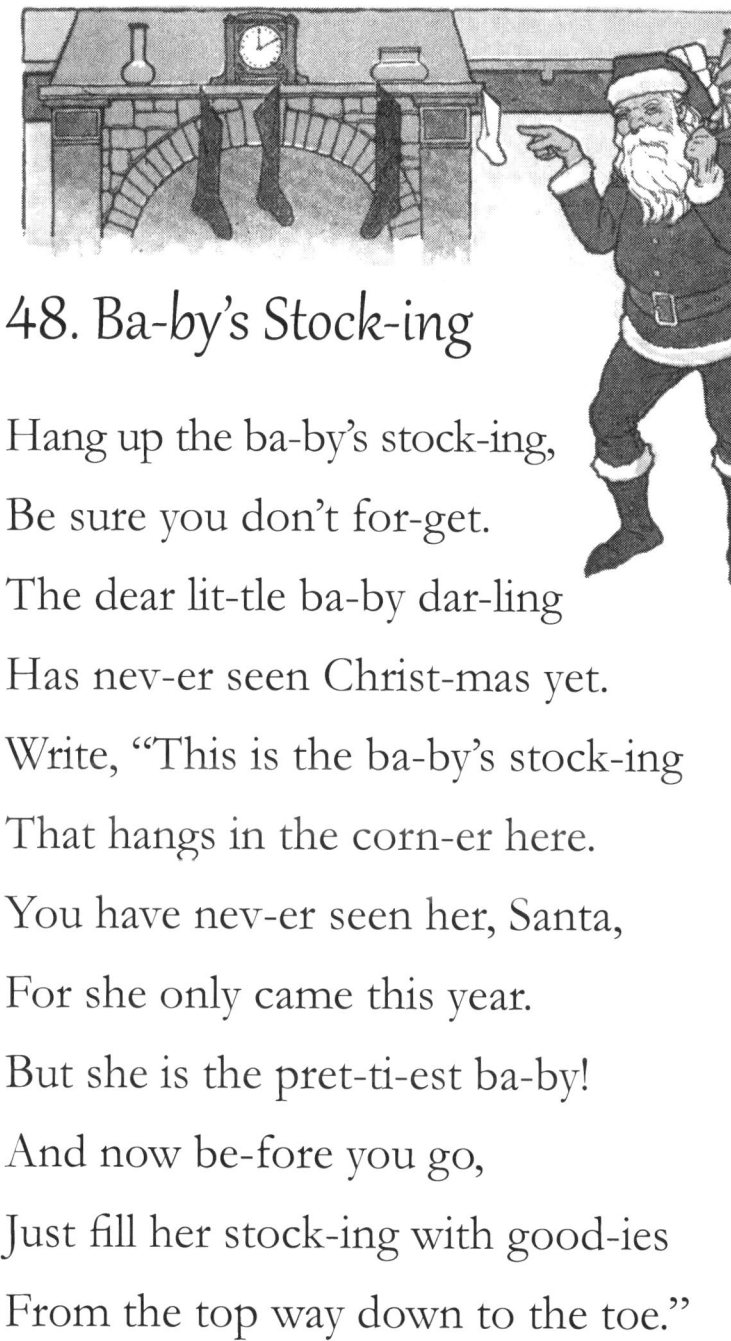

48. Ba-by's Stock-ing

Hang up the ba-by's stock-ing,

Be sure you don't for-get.

The dear lit-tle ba-by dar-ling

Has nev-er seen Christ-mas yet.

Write, "This is the ba-by's stock-ing

That hangs in the corn-er here.

You have nev-er seen her, Santa,

For she only came this year.

But she is the pret-ti-est ba-by!

And now be-fore you go,

Just fill her stock-ing with good-ies

From the top way down to the toe."

49. The Big Man and the Lit-tle Birds

One day a tall man went for a ride.

He was go-ing a-long a coun-try road.

Some friends were with him.

Near the road was an ap-ple tree.

He saw two lit-tle ba-by birds in the road.

They had just tum-bled out of their
nest in the ap-ple tree.

The moth-er bird was fly-ing a-bout,
near them.

But she could not put them in-to
the nest.

"Tweet-tweet, tweet-tweet!" she cried.

She want-ed the men to help her.

"Let us help the bird," said the tall man.

"No, we can-not stop," said his friends.

But the tall man jumped from his horse.

He put the lit-tle birds back in-to
the nest.

"Tweet-tweet, tweet-tweet!" said the
moth-er bird.

She was trying to thank the man.

Then the tall man jumped up on his horse.

He soon caught up with his friends.

"I had to help the bird," he said.

"I could not have slept to-night if I had
not helped her."

The tall man was named
A-bra-ham Lin-coln.

50. Our Flag

There are man-y flags in man-y lands,
    There are flags of ev-er-y hue,
But there is no flag in an-y land
    Like our own Red, White, and Blue.

Then "Hur-rah for the Flag!" our

   coun-try's flag.

   Its stripes and white stars, too;

There is no flag in an-y land

   Like our own Red, White, and Blue.

Mary Howliston.

A-mer-i-ca

My coun-try, 'tis of thee,

Sweet land of Lib-er-ty,

   Of thee I sing;

Land where my fa-thers died,

Land of the pil-grims' pride;

From ev-er-y moun-tain side

   Let Free-dom ring.

Samuel Smith.

51. The Pa-rade on Wash-ing-ton's Birth-day

Grand-fa-ther and Grand-moth-er had a flag.

It was an old, old flag.

It was near-ly as old as Fa-ther.

They gave the flag to Fa-ther.

He loved the old flag.

Pat-ty and Ned loved it, too.

They hung it out of the win-dow ev-er-y Flag day.

One day Fa-ther said, "There will be a pa-rade on George Wash-ing-ton's Birth-day.

It will be a fine pa-rade.

I will take Pat-ty and Ned to see it."

"That will be great fun," said Ned.

The chil-dren jumped for joy.

"Hur-rah! Hur-rah!" they cried.

The great day came at last.

But Fa-ther could not take Ned and
Pat-ty to the pa-rade.

Their Grand-moth-er was sick.

Fa-ther and Moth-er had to go to see her.

Pat-ty and Ned felt ver-y sad.

But they did not cry. Oh, no!

Pat-ty said, "We can-not see the pa-rade.

But we can hang our flag out of
the win-dow."

"Yes," said Ned. "Fa-ther and Moth-er
would like us to do that."

So they hung the flag out of the win-dow.

Soon they heard a great noise.

"Oh, it is the pa-rade!" said Ned.

It is com-ing down our street.

I am so glad our flag is out."

The pa-rade went right by the house.

Ev-er-y one saw the old, old flag.

They said, "Hur-rah for the old, old flag!"

Pat-ty and Ned felt ver-y proud.

Soon Fa-ther and Moth-er came home.

Pat-ty and Ned told them a-bout
the pa-rade.

"Oh! We had a won-der-ful day!"
said Pat-ty.

"Hur-rah for the old, old flag!" said Ned.

"Hur-rah for George Wash-ing-ton!"
said Fa-ther.

Carolyn S. Bailey, Adapted.

52. The Lit-tle Red Hen

A lit-tle red hen once found
a grain of wheat.

"Who will help plant this wheat?"
she asked.

"Not I," said the dog.

"Not I," said the cat.

"Not I," said the pig.

"Not I," said the tur-key.

"Then I will," said the lit-tle red hen.
"Cluck! Cluck!"

So she plant-ed the grain of wheat.

Soon the wheat be-gan to grow.

By and by it grew tall and ripe.

"Who will help reap this wheat?" asked the lit-tle red hen.

"Not I," said the dog.

"Not I," said the cat.

"Not I," said the pig.

"Not I," said the tur-key.

"I will, then," said the lit-tle red hen. "Cluck! Cluck!"

So she reaped the wheat.

"Who will help thresh this wheat?" said the lit-tle red hen.

"Not I," said the dog.

"Not I," said the cat.

"Not I," said the pig.

"Not I," said the tur-key.

"I will, then," said the lit-tle red hen. "Cluck! Cluck!"

So she threshed the wheat.

"Who will help take this wheat to the mill to have it ground?" asked the lit-tle red hen.

"Not I," said the dog.

"Not I," said the cat.

"Not I," said the pig.

"Not I," said the tur-key.

"I will, then," said the lit-tle red hen. "Cluck! Cluck!"

So she took the wheat to the mill.

By and by she came back with the flour.

"Who will help bake a loaf of bread with this flour?" asked the lit-tle red hen.

"Not I," said the dog, the cat, the pig, and the tur-key.

"I will, then," said the lit-tle red hen. "Cluck! Cluck!"

So she baked a loaf of bread with the flour.

"Who will help eat this bread?" asked the lit-tle red hen.

"I will," said the dog.

"I will," said the cat.

"I will," said the pig.

"I will," said the tur-key.

"No, you won't," said the lit-tle red hen.

"My lit-tle chicks and I are go-ing to do that. Cluck! cluck!"

So she called her four lit-tle chicks, and they ate up the loaf of bread.

Old Tale.

53. The Lost Egg

Bob-bie had a pret-ty hen
named Brown-ie.

Brown-ie had a soft nest in the barn.

Can you guess why she sat there so long?

There were ten white eggs un-der her.

By and by Brown-ie heard a "Peep-peep!"

The shells of the eggs were break-ing.

Lit-tle chicks were com-ing out of
the shells.

Soon Brown-ie had nine
lit-tle chicks.

She kept them un-der her
wings, where it was warm.

"Peep, peep, peep!"
said the nine chicks.

"Where is my oth-er chick?"
said Brown-ie.

"I had ten eggs. I see only nine chicks."

"Cluck-cluck, cluck-cluck," said
Brown-ie to her lit-tle chick-ens.

"Let us take a walk."

She took them in-to the gar-den, to
find Bob-bie and his moth-er.

"Oh, Moth-er," cried Bob-bie, "look at
Brown-ie's lit-tle chicks!"

"How man-y has she?" asked
his moth-er.

"I will count them," said Bob-bie.

"One, two, three, four, five, six, sev-en,
eight, nine. There are nine lit-tle chick-ens."

"Why, Bob-bie," said his moth-er, she
had ten eggs. Where is the oth-er chick-en?"

Then his moth-er count-ed them.

She count-ed nine chick-ens, too.

"I will run to the barn," said Bob-bie.

"I may find it there."

A-way he ran as fast as he could go.

There was the egg, right in the nest!

Bob-bie took it up to look at it.

But the egg fell to the ground.

Hark! What did he hear?

"Peep-peep! Peep-peep!"

He looked at the egg and saw a big
crack in the shell.

Then Bob-bie saw an-oth-er
lit-tle chick-en.

He gave it to Brown-ie, and she put it
un-der her wing.

All the oth-er lit-tle chick-ens ran a-bout and flapped their wings.

They were so hap-py!

Brown-ie was hap-py, too. She had found the lost chick.

Norse Folk Tale.

54. The Goats in the Tur-nip Field

Once a boy had three fine goats.

Ev-er-y morn-ing he took them to the hill so that they could eat the green grass.

The goats were ver-y hap-py on the hill.

When eve-ning came, the boy would take them home.

Once they ran in-to a tur-nip field.

They boy could not get them out.

What do you think he did?

He sat down and cried.

A-long came a rab-bit, hop, hop, hop.

"Why are you cry-ing?" asked the rab-bit.

"Oh, oh! I can-not get my goats out of the tur-nip field," said the boy.

"I will do it for you," said the rab-bit.

So he ran af-ter the goats.

But he could not get them out.

Then the rab-bit sat down and cried.

Soon a fox came a-long.

"Rab-bit, why are you cry-ing?" asked the fox.

"I cry be-cause the boy cries," he said.

"The boy cries be-cause he can-not get his goats out of the tur-nip field."

"I will do it for him," said the fox.

So the fox ran af-ter the goats.

But he could not get them out.

Then the fox sat down and cried.

As they were cry-ing, a wolf came by.

"Fox, why are you cry-ing?" said the wolf.

"I cry be-cause the rab-bit cries," said the fox.

"The rab-bit cries be-cause the boy cries.

The boy cries be-cause he can-not get his goats out of the tur-nip field."

"I will do it for him," said the wolf.

So the wolf ran af-ter the goats.

But he could not get them out.

Then the wolf sat down and cried, too.

A lit-tle bee saw them all cry-ing.

"Wolf, why are you cry-ing?" said the bee.

"I cry be-cause the fox cries," said the wolf.

"The fox cries be-cause the rab-bit cries.

The rab-bit cries be-cause the boy cries.

The boy cries be-cause he can-not get his goats out of the tur-nip field."

"I will do it for him," said the bee.

Then they all stopped cry-ing and be-gan to laugh. "Ha, ha! Ha, ha, ha!" they said.

"How can a lit-tle bee like you do it?"

But the bee flew in-to the tur-nip field.

He flew right to a big goat's back.

"Buzz-z-z!" he said, and out the goats ran!

Do you know why they ran out so fast?

They ran all the way home, too.

The boy laughed and ran af-ter them.

Norwegian Folk Tale.

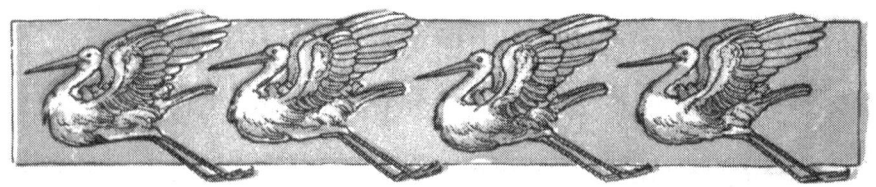

55. The Kind Cranes

Six hun-gry lit-tle birds once sat by the sea.

"Let us cross the sea," said one.

"We can get fat worms o-ver there."

"But the sea is so wide!" said an-oth-er. "How can we get a-cross?"

Soon a fish came a-long.

"Fish, will you take us a-cross the sea?" asked the lit-tle birds.

"I will take you down in-to the sea!" said the fish.

"We will go just like this!"

And he swam down, down, down, in-to the sea.

"Dear, dear!" said the lit-tle birds.

"Dear, dear! Let us wait."

So the hung-ry lit-tle birds wait-ed.

By and by a sheep came walk-ing a-long.

"Sheep, will you take us a-cross the sea?" asked the lit-tle birds.

"I nev-er swim," said the sheep, "and I can-not fly.

Why don't you wait for the cranes?"

"Who are they?" asked the lit-tle birds.

"They are great, big birds," said the sheep.

"Their wings are so strong that they can fly a-cross the sea.

They have long beaks and long necks.

They have long legs and big backs.

The cranes are ver-y kind.

Ev-er-y year they take oth-er lit-tle birds a-cross the sea.

They will take you, too."

So the hun-gry lit-tle birds wait-ed.

By and by four cranes came fly-ing a-long.

The lit-tle birds called to the first crane, "Will you take us a-cross the sea?

We can get some fat worms o-ver there."

"My back is full of lit-tle birds now," said the first crane. "Ask the last crane.

He can take you a-cross."

So the lit-tle birds called to the last crane, "Will you take us a-cross the sea?"

"Yes, I will take you," he said.

"My back is near-ly full.

See all the lit-tle birds on it!

But you are so lit-tle that I can find a place for you. Hop on!"

The six lit-tle birds hopped on-to his back.

The oth-er birds made a place for them.

"Are you all right?" asked the crane.

"Here we go, lit-tle birds."

The lit-tle birds held on with their beaks and their claws.

A-way they flew, a-cross the wide, wide sea.

They found all the worms they could eat.

And the six lit-tle birds got fat-ter and fat-ter.

Old Tale.

56. The North Wind

"The North Wind is cold,"
    The Rob-ins say;
"And that is the rea-son
    We fly a-way."

"The North Wind is cold;
    He is com-ing, hark!
I must haste a-way,"
    Says the Mead-ow Lark.

The North Wind is cold
    And brings the snow,"
Says Jen-ny Wren,
    "And I must go."

"The North Wind is cold
    As cold can be,
But I'm not a-fraid,"
    Says the Chick-a-dee.

So the Chick-a-dee stays
    And sees the snow,
And likes to hear
    The North Wind blow.

Rebecca B. Foresman.

57. What Does Lit-tle Bird-ie Say?

What does lit-tle bird-ie say,

In her nest at peep of day?

Let me fly, says lit-tle bird-ie,

Moth-er, let me fly a-way.

Bird-ie, rest a lit-tle long-er

Till the lit-tle wings are strong-er.

So she rests a lit-tle long-er,

Then she flies a-way.

What does lit-tle ba-by say,

    In her bed at peep of day?

Ba-by says, like lit-tle bird-ie,

    Let me rise and fly a-way.

Ba-by, sleep a lit-tle long-er,

    Till the lit-tle limbs are strong-er.

If she sleeps a lit-tle long-er,

    Ba-by too shall fly a-way.

Alfred, Lord Tennyson.

58. The Hen and the Squir-rel

One day a hen met a squir-rel.

"Friend Hen," said the squir-rel, "do you see that tall oak tree?

It is full of good a-corns.

Let us get some to eat."

"All right, friend Squir-rel," said the hen.

So they ran to the tree.

The squir-rel ran right up the tree and ate an a-corn.

"How good it is!" he said.

The hen tried to fly up get an a-corn.

But she could not fly so high.

So she called up to the squir-rel,

"Friend Squir-rel, give me an a-corn."

The squir-rel found a big a-corn.

He threw it down to her.

The a-corn hit the hen, and cut her head.

So she ran to an old wo-man and said,

"Old Wo-man, please give me a soft cloth.

Then I can tie up my poor head."

"First give me two hairs," said the old wo-man.

"Then I will give you a soft cloth."

The hen ran to a dog.

"Good Dog, give me two hairs," she said.

"I will give them to the old wo-man.

The old wo-man will give me a soft cloth.

Then I can tie up my poor head."

"First give me some bread," said the dog.

"Then I will give you two hairs."

The hen went to a bak-er and said,

"Oh, Good Bak-er, give me some bread.

I will give the bread to the dog.

The dog will give me two hairs.

I will give the hairs to the old wo-man.

The old wo-man will give me a soft cloth.

Then I can tie up my poor head."

"First get me some wood," said the bak-er.

"Then I will give you some bread."

The hen went to the for-est and said,

"Oh, Good For-est, give me some wood.

I will give the wood to the bak-er.

The bak-er will give me some bread.

I will give the bread to the dog.

The dog will give me two hairs.

I will give the hairs to the old wo-man.

The old wo-man will give me a soft cloth.

Then I can tie up my poor head."

"First give me some wa-ter," said
the for-est.

"Then I will give you wood."

The hen went to a brook.

"Brook, give me some wa-ter.

I will give it to the for-est.

The for-est will give me wood.

I will give the wood to the bak-er.

The bak-er will give me bread.

I will give the bread to the dog.

The dog will give me two hairs.

I will give them to the old wo-man.

The old wo-man will give me a soft cloth.

Then I can tie up my poor head."

The brook gave the hen wa-ter.

She gave the wa-ter to the for-est.

The for-est gave her some wood.

She gave the wood to the bak-er.

The bak-er gave her some bread.

She gave the bread to the dog.

The dog gave her two hairs.

She gave the two hairs to the old wo-man.

The old wo-man gave her a soft cloth.

So the hen tied up her poor head.

Old Tale.

59. The Pine Tree and Its Nee-dles

A lit-tle pine tree lived in the woods.

It had leaves like long green nee-dles.

But the lit-tle pine tree was not hap-py.

"I do not like my green nee-dles," it said.

"I wish I had beau-ti-ful leaves.

How hap-py I should be if I only had gold leaves!"

Night came.

Then the Fair-y of the Trees walked in the woods.

"Lit-tle pine tree," she said, "you may have your wish."

In the morn-ing the lit-tle pine tree had leaves of gold.

"How beau-ti-ful I am!" it said.

"See how I shine in the sun!

Now I am hap-py!"

Night came.

Then a man walked in the woods.

He took all the gold leaves and put them in-to a bag.

The lit-tle tree had no leaves at all.

"What shall I do?" it said.

"I do not want gold leaves a-gain.

I wish I had glass leaves.

Glass leaves would shine in the sun, too.

And no one would take glass leaves."

Night came.

The Fair-y walked in the woods a-gain.

"Lit-tle pine tree," she said, "you may have your wish."

In the morn-ing the tree had glass leaves.

"How beau-ti-ful I am!" it said.

"See how I shine in the sun!

Now I am hap-py."

Night came.

Then the wind came through the woods.

Oh, how it blew!

It broke all the beau-ti-ful glass leaves.

"What shall I do now?" said the tree.

"I do not want glass leaves a-gain.

The oak tree has big green leaves.

I wish I had big green leaves, too."

Night came.

Then the Fair-y of the Trees walked in the woods a-gain.

"Lit-tle pine tree," she said, "you may have your wish."

In the morn-ing the lit-tle pine tree had big green leaves.

"How beau-ti-ful I am!" it said.

"Now I am like the oth-er trees.

At last I am hap-py."

Night came.

A goat came through the woods.

He ate all the big green leaves.

"What shall I do?" said the tree.

"A man took my leaves of gold.

The wind broke my leaves of glass.

A goat ate my big green leaves.

I wish I had my long nee-dles a-gain."

Night came.

The Fair-y walked in the woods a-gain.

"Lit-tle pine tree," she said, "you may have your wish."

In the morn-ing the lit-tle pine tree had its long nee-dles a-gain.

"Now I am hap-py," said the tree.

"I do not want an-y oth-er leaves.

Lit-tle pine nee-dles are best for lit-tle pine trees."

Old Tale.

60. How Gos-ling Learned to Swim

One day Lit-tle Gos-ling went in-to a pond.

"Why do you go in-to the pond?" asked the chick-en.

"I am go-ing to learn to swim," said Lit-tle Gos-ling.

"Then I will peep," said the chick-en.

So the chick-en peeped.

"Why do you peep?" asked the duck-ling.

"Lit-tle Gos-ling swims, so I peep," said the chick-en.

"Then I will quack," said the duck-ling. So the duck-ling quacked.

"Why do you quack?" asked the rab-bit.

"Lit-tle Gos-ling swims, the chick-en peeps, so I quack," said the duck-ling.

"Then I will leap," said the rabbit.

So the rab-bit leaped.

"Why do you leap?" asked the black colt.

"Lit-tle Gos-ling swims, the chick-en peeps,

The duck-ling quacks, so I leap," said the rab-bit.

"Then I will run," said the black colt. So the black colt ran.

"Why do you run?" asked the white dove.

"Lit-tle Gos-ling swims, the chick-en peeps,

The duck-ling quacks and the rab-bit leaps.

So I run," said the black colt.

"Then I will coo," said the white dove.
So the white dove cooed.

"Lit-tle Gos-ling swims, the
chick-en peeps,

The duck-ling quacks and the
rab-bit leaps.

The black colt runs, so I coo," said the
white dove.

"Then I will bark," said the brown dog.

So the brown dog barked.

"Why do you bark?" said the
yel-low calf.

"Lit-tle Gos-ling swims, the
chick-en peeps,

The duck-ling quacks and the
rab-bit leaps.

The black colt runs and the white
dove coos,

So I bark," said the brown dog.

"Then I will moo," said the yel-low calf.

So Lit-tle Gos-ling swam and the
chick-en peeped,

The duck-ling quacked and the
rab-bit leaped,

The black colt ran and the white
dove cooed,

The brown dog barked and the
yel-low calf mooed.

And Lit-tle Gos-ling learned
to swim.

English Folk Tale.

61. 1 Don't Care

A horse and a brown colt once lived in a mead-ow.

One day the gate was o-pen.

"I will run out of the gate," said the brown colt.

"No, no!" said the horse.

"You must stay in the mead-ow."

"Why?" asked the brown colt.

"I do not know," said the horse.

"But the old white horse told me to stay. So I shall stay."

"I don't care!" said the colt.

"I do not like it here.

If I run down the road, I shall have more fun."

So off he ran, down the road.

By and by he met the old white horse.

"Why are you here?" asked the old horse.

"I want some fun," said the colt.

"I am tired of stay-ing in the mead-ow."

"The mead-ow is the best place for you," said the old white horse.

"You are safe in the mead-ow.

You are too lit-tle to see the world."

"I don't care!" said the brown colt.

He shook his head and ran on.

By and by he met a mule.

The mule was pulling a big cart.

"Why are you here?" he asked the colt.

"You should be in the mead-ow.

The town is close by, and it is no place for a lit-tle colt like you."

"I don't care! I want some fun," said the brown colt.

The colt ran on un-til he came to the town.

He had nev-er seen a town be-fore.

What a noise the carts made!

The lit-tle colt was fright-ened.

He want-ed to run back to the mead-ow.

Then some men and boys ran af-ter him.

They shout-ed at him and tried to catch him.

Soon he came to a big glass win-dow.

He saw his shad-ow in the win-dow, and he thought it was an-oth-er colt.

"Oh, there is an-oth-er colt just like me!" said the lit-tle brown colt.

"I will ask him the way to the mead-ow."

But it was not an-oth-er colt.

It was only his shad-ow he saw in the glass.

The lit-tle brown colt ran in-to the win dow and broke the glass.

The glass cut him, and he fell down.

Then some men caught him.

They took the lit-tle colt back to the mead-ow and shut him in.

Now he does not want to run a-way.

He nev-er says, "I don't care" an-y-more.

Gertrude Sellon.

62. The Cam-el and the Pig

One day a cam-el and a pig
were talk-ing.

The cam-el was proud be-cause he
was tall.

But the pig was proud be-cause he
was short.

"Just look at me!" said the cam-el.

"See how tall I am!

It is bet-ter to be tall, like me."

"Oh, no!" said the pig.

"Just look at me!

See how short I am!

It is bet-ter to be short, like me."

"If I am not right, I will give up my hump," said the cam-el.

"If I am not right, I will give up my snout," said the pig.

Soon they came to a gar-den.

All a-round it was a wall.

There was no gate in the wall.

The cam-el was so tall that he could see o-ver the wall. He could see fine, ripe fruit in the gar-den.

His neck was so long that he could reach o-ver the wall and get the fruit.

He ate all he want-ed.

But the poor pig was short.

He could not reach o-ver the wall.

He could not get in-side, be-cause there was no gate.

"Ha, ha, ha!" laughed the cam-el.

"Now would you rath-er be tall or short?"

Soon they came to an-oth-er gar-den.

All a-round it was a high wall.

It was so high that the cam-el could not see o-ver it.

But there was a gate in the wall.

The pig went through the gate.

This gar-den was full of fine, ripe fruit, too.

The pig ate all he want-ed.

But the cam-el was so tall that he could not get through the gate.

"Ha, ha, ha!" laughed the pig.

"Now would you rath-er be tall or short?"

So the cam-el kept his hump, and the pig kept his snout.

For they said,

"Some-times it's bet-ter to be tall,

And some-times it's bet-ter to be small."

A Tale from India.

63. The Lit-tle Roos-ter

Once there was a man who had a lit-tle roos-ter.

The lit-tle roos-ter liked to crow.

One night the man said, "How sleep-y I am! I will go to bed and have a good sleep."

So he went to bed, and slept.

Next morn-ing the lit-tle roos-ter got up ver-y ear-ly and ran to the house.

He flapped his wings and crowed, "Cock-a-doo-dle-doo!"

He crowed so loud that he woke the man.

"That must be the lit-tle roos-ter," said the man.

The man was so ang-ry that he threw his hair-brush at the lit-tle roos-ter.

The roos-ter ran a-way as fast as he could.

Then the man said, "Now that I am up, I will plant my gar-den."

So he plant-ed his gar-den.

That night he put the lit-tle roos-ter in-to the hen yard.

He said, "Now I will have a long sleep."

He went to bed, and slept.

But the lit-tle roos-ter got up ver-y ear-ly the next morn-ing.

He flew out of the hen yard and ran to the house.

"Cock-a-doo-dle-doo!" he crowed.

The man woke up and said, "There is that lit-tle roos-ter a-gain."

He was so ang-ry that he threw his comb at the roos-ter.

But the lit-tle roos-ter had a comb. So he ran a-way as fast as he could.

Then the man said, "Now that I am up, I will weed my gar-den."

So he weed-ed his gar-den.

That night the man tied the lit-tle roos-ter in the hen yard with a string.

He said, "Now I will have a long sleep."

So he went to bed, and slept.

The lit-tle roos-ter got up ver-y ear-ly the next morn-ing.

He bit the string in two and flew out of the hen yard.

He ran to the house and flapped his wings.

"Cock-a-doo-dle-doo!" he crowed.

The lit-tle roos-ter crowed so loud that the man woke up.

"There is that lit-tle roos-ter a-gain!" said the man. "How can I sleep?"

He was as ang-ry as he could be.

So he caught the lit-tle roos-ter and gave him a-way.

That night the man went to sleep ear-ly.

He had a long sleep.

The next night he had a long sleep.

And the next night.

And the next.

And the next.

But the weeds grew up and filled his gar-den.

Charles Battell Loomis, Adapted.

64. North Wind at Play

North Wind went out one sum-mer day.

"Now I will have a good play," he said.

He saw an ap-ple tree full of ap-ples.

"Oh, ap-ple tree, come and play with me!

We can have fun to-geth-er," said

North Wind.

"Oh, no!" said the ap-ple tree.

"I can-not play with you. I must work.

I am helping my ap-ples to grow.

By and by they will grow big and red.

Then lit-tle chil-dren can eat them.

Oh, no! I can-not play with you."

"We will see a-bout that," said
North Wind.

"I will make you play with me."

"Puff! Puff!" he said, and all the
ap-ples fell to the ground.

Then North Wind saw a field of corn.

"Oh, corn, come and play with me!"
he said.

"No, no, North Wind!" said the corn.

"I can-not play with you just now.

I must stand still and grow.

Look un-der my long, green leaves.

Do you see the white grains un-der them?

They must grow big and yel-low.

Then they can be ground at the mill.

Lit-tle chil-dren can have corn bread
to eat.

No, no! I can-not play with you."

"Puff! Puff!" said North Wind.

All the corn fell to the ground.

By and by North Wind saw a lil-y.

"Oh, lil-y, come and play with me.

We can have fun to-geth-er," he said.

"Oh, no, North Wind!" said the lil-y.

"I can-not play with you to-day.

I must take care of my buds.

They will o-pen soon and then they will
be beau-ti-ful lil-ies.

Then lit-tle chil-dren will come to see me.

Oh, no! I can-not play with you."

"Puff! Puff!" said North Wind.

The lil-y hung her head.

She could not look up a-gain.

At night North Wind went home.

"What did you do to-day?" said his fa-ther.

"I went out to play," said North Wind.

"But no one want-ed to play with me.

So I shook the ap-ple tree, and all the ap-ples fell to the ground.

Then I shook the corn, and it fell, too.

I blew un-til the lil-y hung her head.

I did not want to hurt them, Fa-ther. I was only play-ing."

"You are too rough," said his fa-ther.

"I know you do not want to be rough.

You must stay at home in sum-mer.

You must wait un-til the ap-ples and the corn and the lil-ies are gone.

You may go out to play in win-ter.

Then you can puff all you want to."

Old Tale.

65. Three Bil-ly Goats Gruff

Once there were three bil-ly goats.

They were all named "Gruff."

Ev-er-y day they went up a hill to eat the grass and grow fat.

They had to go o-ver a lit-tle brook be-fore they came to the hill.

O-ver the brook was a bridge.

A Troll lived un-der the bridge.

He was so big and cross that ev-er-y one was a-fraid of him.

One day the three bil-ly goats were go-ing up the hill to get fat.

Lit-tle Bil-ly Goat Gruff was the first to cross the bridge.

Trip-trap! Trip-trap! went the bridge.

"Who is that trip-trap-ping on my bridge?" called the Troll.

"Oh, it is just Lit-tle Bil-ly Goat Gruff.

I am go-ing up the hill to get fat," said the lit-tle bil-ly goat.

"Well, I am com-ing to gob-ble you up!" said the Troll.

"Oh, no!" said Lit-tle Bil-ly Goat.

"Do not take me! I am too lit-tle.

Wait for Sec-ond Bil-ly Goat.

He is big-ger than I am."

"Well, be off with you!" said the Troll.

Soon Sec-ond Bil-ly Goat Gruff came to the bridge.

Trip-trap! Trip-trap! Trip-trap! went the bridge.

"Who is that trip-trap-ping on my bridge!" called the Troll.

"Oh, it is just Sec-ond Bil-ly Goat Gruff.

I am go-ing up the hill to get fat," said the sec-ond bil-ly goat.

"Well, I am com-ing to gob-ble you up!" said the Troll.

"Oh, no!" said Sec-ond Bil-ly Goat.

"Do not take me.

I am not ver-y big.

Wait for Big Bil-ly Goat.

He is big-ger than I am."

"Well, be off with you!" said the Troll.

Just then Big Bil-ly Goat Gruff came to the bridge.

Trip-trap! Trip-trap! Trip-trap! Trip-trap! went the bridge.

"Who is that trip-trap-ping on my bridge?" called the Troll.

"Oh, it is just Big Bil-ly Goat Gruff. I am go-ing up the hill to get fat."

"Well, I am com-ing to gob-ble you up!" said the Troll.

"Come a-long, then, Troll!" said Big Bil-ly Goat Gruff.

So the Troll came a-long.

Big Bil-ly Goat Gruff flew at him.

He caught the Troll on his horns and threw him in-to the brook.

The Troll was fright-ened.

He jumped out of the wa-ter and ran a-way.

The three bil-ly goats nev-er saw him a-gain.

They go up the hill ev-er-y day, and now they are as fat as they can be.

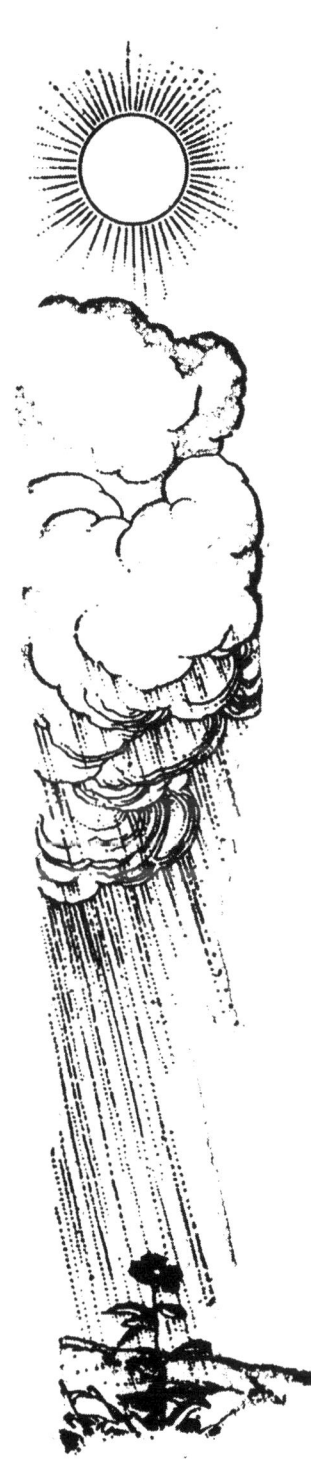

66. The Lit-tle Plant

In the heart of a seed
    Bur-ied deep, so deep,
A dear lit-tle plant
    Lay fast a-sleep.

"Wake!" said the sun-shine,
    "And creep to the light,"
"Wake!" said the voice
    Of the rain-drops bright.

The lit-tle plant heard,
    And it rose to see
What the won-der-ful
    Out-side world might be.

Kate Louise Brown.

67. The Swing

How do you like to go up in a swing,
    Up in the air so blue?
Oh, I do think it the pleas-ant-est thing
    Ev-er a child can do!

Up in the air and o-ver the wall,
    Till I can see so wide,
Riv-ers and trees and cat-tle and all
    O-ver the coun-try-side.

Till I look down on the gar-den green,
    Down on the roof so brown—
Up in the air I go fly-ing a-gain,
    Up in the air and down!

Robert Louis Stevenson.

68. The Sleep-ing Ap-ple

A lit-tle ap-ple hung high up on an ap-ple tree.

It slept and grew, and slept and grew.

At last it was big and ripe, but it still slept on.

One day a lit-tle girl came walk-ing un-der the tree and saw the ap-ple.

"Why does the ap-ple sleep so long?" said the lit-tle girl.

"The world is so beau-ti-ful!

I wish the ap-ple would wake up and see.

Maybe I can wake it."

So she called out, "Oh, ap-ple, wake up! Do not sleep so long.

Wake up, wake up, and come with me!"

But the sleep-ing ap-ple did not wake.

"Oh, Sun, beau-ti-ful Sun!" said the girl.

"Will you kiss the ap-ple and make it wake? That is the way moth-er wakes me."

"Oh, yes," said the sun, "indeed I will."

So he kissed the ap-ple un-til it was a gold-en yel-low.

It was as gold-en as the sun.

But still the ap-ple slept on.

By and by a rob-in flew to the tree.

"Dear Rob-in," said the lit-tle girl, "can you help me wake the sleep-ing ap-ple?

I can-not wake it, and the sun can-not wake it. We have tried and tried.

It will sleep too long."

"Oh, yes, lit-tle girl, I can wake the ap-ple," said the rob-in.

"I will sing to it just as I sing to my lit-tle bird-ies in their nest.

I wake my bird-ies ev-er-y morn-ing with a song."

"Cheer up! Wake up! Cheer up! Wake up!" sang the rob-in in the ap-ple tree.

But the sleep-ing ap-ple did not wake.

"Oo—oo—oo! Oo—oo—oo!"

"Who is that com-ing through the trees?" said the lit-tle girl.

"Oh, it is my friend, the Wind. Oh, Wind, you wake me some-times at night.

Can you not wake this beau-ti-ful ap-ple? It has slept so long."

"Indeed I can," said the wind.

"It is time for all ap-ples to wake up. Sum-mer will soon be o-ver."

"Oo—oo—oo!" he said, and shook the tree.

The ap-ple woke and fell down, down, down to the ground.

The lit-tle girl kissed its gold-en cheeks.

"Oh, thank you, kind wind," she said.

"If you had not come, the ap-ple would have slept all the sum-mer long."

Folk Tale.

69. Sweet Por-ridge

Once there was a lit-tle girl who lived with her moth-er.

They were ver-y poor.

Some-times they had no sup-per.

Then they went to bed hung-ry.

One day the lit-tle girl went in-to the woods.

She want-ed wood for the fire.

She was so hun-gry and sad!

"Oh, I wish I had some sweet por-ridge!" she said.

"I wish I had a pot full for moth-er and me.

We could eat it all up."

Just then she saw an old wo-man with a lit-tle black pot.

She said, "Lit-tle girl, why are you so sad?"

"I am hun-gry," said the lit-tle girl.

"My moth-er is hungry, too.

We have noth-ing to eat.

Oh, I wish we had some sweet por-ridge for our sup-per!"

"I will help you," said the old wo-man.

"Take this lit-tle black pot.

When you want some sweet por-ridge, you must say, 'Lit-tle pot, boil!'

The lit-tle pot will boil and boil and boil.

You will have all the sweet por-ridge you want.

When the lit-tle pot is full, you must say, 'Lit-tle pot, stop!'

Then the lit-tle pot will stop boil-ing."

The lit-tle girl thanked the old wo-man, and ran home with the lit-tle black pot.

Then she made a fire with the wood and put the lit-tle black pot on the fire.

"Lit-tle pot, boil!" she said.

The lit tle pot boiled and boiled and boiled, until it was full of sweet por-ridge.

Then the lit-tle girl said, "Lit-tle pot, stop!"

The lit-tle pot stopped boil-ing.

She called her moth-er, and they ate all the sweet por-ridge they want-ed.

The lit-tle girl told her moth-er a-bout the old wo-man.

"Now," they said, "we are hap-py.

We shall not be hun-gry an-y-more."

The next day the lit-tle girl went in-to the woods a-gain.

She was gone a long time.

"She will be hun-gry when she comes home," said her moth-er.

"I will boil the sweet por-ridge."

So she put the lit-tle black pot on the fire.

"Lit-tle pot, boil!" she said.

The lit-tle pot boiled and boiled un-til it was full of sweet por-ridge.

The moth-er want-ed the pot to stop boil-ing.

But she for-got what to say.

The pot boiled and boiled.

The por-ridge boiled o-ver on-to the stove.

It ran all o-ver the stove.

Then it ran all o-ver the floor.

It flowed in-to the street.

It flowed on and on and on.

The peo-ple all ran out of their houses.

"Oh! Oh! Oh!" they cried.

"The sea has turned to por-ridge!

It is flow-ing o-ver the world!

What shall we do?"

No one knew how to make the lit-tle black pot stop boil-ing.

Af-ter a long time the lit-tle girl came home.

The pot was boil-ing and boil-ing.

"Lit-tle pot, stop!" said the lit-tle girl.

And the lit-tle pot stopped.

But for man-y days af-ter that the street was full of sweet por-ridge.

When peo-ple want-ed to get to the oth-er side, they had to eat their way a-cross.

Folk Tale.

70. John-ny Cake

Once there were a lit-tle old man, a lit-tle old wo-man, and a lit-tle boy.

One day the old wo-man made a round John-ny cake.

She put it in-to the stove to bake.

She said to the lit-tle boy, "You must bake the John-ny cake for us.

We will eat it for sup-per."

Then the lit-tle old man took a spade, and the lit-tle old wo-man took a hoe.

They went to work in the gar-den.

The lit-tle boy was all a-lone in the house.

He for-got a-bout the John-ny cake.

All at once he heard a great noise.

The stove door flew o-pen, and John-ny cake rolled out.

Out of the house he rolled.

The lit-tle boy ran to the gar-den.

"Fa-ther! Moth-er!" he called.

"John-ny cake is roll-ing a-way."

The lit-tle old man threw down his spade, and the lit-tle old wo-man threw down her hoe.

Then they all ran as fast as they could af-ter John-ny cake.

But they could not catch him.

John-ny cake laughed and said,

"I am having some fun;

I roll and they run;

I can beat ev-er-y one."

He rolled on and on.

Soon he came to a hen.

"John-ny cake, where are you go-ing?"
asked the hen.

"Oh, I am out roll-ing," he said.

"I have rolled a-way from

A lit-tle old man,

A lit tle old wo man,

A lit-tle boy,

And I can roll a-way from you, too!"

"You can, can you?" said the hen.

"We will see a-bout that!

I think I will just eat you up!"

So the hen ran as fast as she could.

But she could not catch John-ny cake.

John-ny cake laughed and said,

"I am having some fun;

I roll and they run;

I can beat ev-er-y one."

He rolled on and on.

By and by he came to a cow.

"John-ny cake, where are you go-ing?"

asked the cow.

"Oh, I am out roll-ing," he said.

"I have rolled a-way from

A lit-tle old man,

A lit-tle old wo-man,

A lit-tle boy,

And a hen.

I can roll a-way from you, too!"

"You can, can you?" said the cow.

"I think I will just eat you up!"

The cow ran as fast as she could.

But she could not catch him.

John-ny cake laughed and said,

"I am having some fun;

I roll and they run;

I can beat ev-er-y one."

He rolled on un-til he came to a pig.

The pig was ly-ing down.

"Where are you go-ing?" asked the pig.

"Oh, I am out roll-ing," said
John-ny cake.

"I have rolled a-way from

A lit-tle old man,

A lit-tle old wo-man,

A lit-tle boy,

A hen,

And a cow.

I can roll a-way from you, too!"

"Woof, woof! I am sleep-y," said the pig.

John-ny cake went near to him.

"I will make you hear me!" he said.

"I have rolled a-way from

A lit-tle old man,

A lit-tle old wo-man,

A lit-tle boy,

A hen,

And a cow.

I can roll a-way from you, too!"

"Woof, woof!" said the pig.

"I am sleep-y. Go a-way!"

He shut his eyes.

John-ny cake got as near to the pig as he could.

He shout-ed at him.

"Do you hear me?" he called.

"I have rolled a-way from

A lit-tle old man,

A lit-tle old wo-man,

A lit-tle boy,

A hen,

And a cow.

I can roll a-way from you, too!"

The pig o-pened his eyes.

He o-pened his mouth, too.

He caught John-ny cake, and ate him up.

English Folk Tale.

71. Ma-ry and the Lark

Ma-ry: Good morn-ing, pret-ty lark.

Have you an-y bird-ies in that nest?

Lark: Oh, yes. I have three bird-ies here.

They are ver-y beau-ti-ful, and they

are ver-y good, too.

Ma-ry: May I see them, pret-ty lark?

Lark: Oh, yes. Come here, lit-tle ones.

This is Ti-ny Beak, this is Light

Wing, and this is Bright Eyes.

Ma-ry: How beau-ti-ful they are!

There are three chil-dren in our

home, too, Al-ice, Ned, and I.

Moth-er says we are ver-y good.

We know how much she loves us.

Bright Eyes: Moth-er loves us, too.

Ma-ry: I am sure she does.

Pret-ty lark, may I take Ti-ny Beak

home to play with me?

Lark: Yes, you may take Ti-ny Beak

home with you, if you will bring

ba-by Al-ice to us.

Ma-ry: Oh, no, no! I can-not do that.

Ba-by Al-ice can-not leave moth-er.

She is so lit-tle!

She would not like to live out

of doors, and she is too big for

your lit-tle nest.

Lark: But Ti-ny Beak can-not leave

his moth-er.

He is such a lit-tle bird.

He is too lit-tle for your big house.

He loves his lit-tle round nest the best.

Ti-ny Beak: Chirp, chirp, chirp! So I do!

Ma-ry: Poor lit-tle Ti-ny Beak!

I will not take you.

I see that your lit-tle round nest is

best for you.

Lark: North and South

and East and West,

Each one loves his

own home best.

Ma-ry: Good-bye, bird-ies! Good-bye!

Light Wing: Good-bye, Ma-ry!

Come to see us a-gain soon.

72. The Hen Who Went to High Dov-er

I

Once a hen was in the woods.

When night came she flew up in-to an oak tree and went to sleep.

Soon she had a dream.

She dreamed that she would find a nest of gold-en eggs if she went to High Dov-er.

She woke up with a jump.

"I must go to High Dov-er," she said.

"I must find the nest of gold-en eggs."

So she flew out of the tree and went up the road.

When she had gone a lit-tle way, she met a roos-ter.

"Good-day, Cock-y Lock-y!" said the hen.

"Good-day, Hen-ny Pen-ny!

Where are you go-ing so ear-ly?" said the roos-ter.

"I am go-ing to High Dov-er. I shall find a nest of gold-en eggs there," said the hen.

"Who told you that, Hen-ny Pen-ny?" asked the roos-ter.

"I sat in the oak tree last night and dreamed it," said the hen.

"I will go with you," said the roos-ter.

So they went a long way to-geth-er un-til they met a duck.

"Good-day, Duck-y Luck-y!" said the roos-ter.

"Good-day, Cock-y Lock-y! Where are you go-ing so ear-ly?" asked the duck.

"I am go-ing to High Dov-er. I shall find a nest of gold-en eggs there," said the roos-ter.

"Who told you that, Cock-y Lock-y?" asked the duck.

"Hen-ny Pen-ny!" said the roos-ter.

"Who told you that, Hen-ny Pen-ny?" asked the duck.

"I sat in the oak tree last night and dreamed it," said the hen.

"I will go with you!" said the duck.

So they went a long way to-geth-er un-til they met a gan-der.

"Good-day, Gan-dy Pan-dy!" said the duck.

"Good-day, Duck-y Luck-y!" said the gan-der. "Where are you go-ing so ear-ly?"

"I am go-ing to High Dov-er. I shall find a nest of gold-en eggs there," said the duck.

"Who told you that, Duck-y Luck-y?" asked the gan-der.

"Cock-y Lock-y."

"Who told you that, Cock-y Lock-y?"

"Hen-ny Pen-ny."

"How do you know that, Hen-ny Pen-ny?" asked the gan-der.

"I sat in the oak tree last night and dreamed it," said the hen.

"I will go with you!" said the gan-der.

So they went a long way to-geth-er un-til they met a fox.

"Good-day, Fox-y Wox-y!" said the gan-der.

"Good-day, Gan-dy Pan-dy! Where are you go-ing so ear-ly?" asked the fox.

"I am go-ing to High Dov-er. I shall find a nest of gold-en eggs there," said the gan-der.

"Who told you that, Gan-dy Pan-dy?"

"Duck-y Luck-y."

"Who told you that, Duck-y Luck-y?" asked the fox.

"Cock-y Lock-y."

"Who told you that, Cock-y Lock-y?"

"Hen-ny Pen-ny."

"How do you know that, Hen-ny Pen-ny?"

"I sat in the oak tree last night and dreamed it, Fox-y Wox-y," said the hen.

"How fool-ish you are!" said the fox.

"There is no nest of gold-en eggs at High Dov-er.

You are cold and tired.

Come with me to my warm den."

So they all went with the fox to his den.

They all got warm and sleep-y.

The duck and the gan-der went to sleep in a corn-er.

But the roos-ter and the hen slept on a roost.

When they were a-sleep, the fox ate the gan-der and the duck.

Just then the hen woke up.

She saw Cock-y Lock-y near her.

She looked for Gan-dy Pan-dy and Duck-y Luck-y.

She could not see them, but she saw feath-ers on the floor!

"I must fool the fox," she said.

So she looked up the chim-ney.

"Oh! Oh!" she called to the fox.

"Look at the geese fly-ing by!"

The fox ran out to see the geese. He want-ed some geese to eat.

Then Hen-ny Pen-ny woke up Cock-y Lock-y.

She told him what she had seen.

"Fly! Fly!" she cried.

"Let us get out of here!"

So Cock-y Lock-y and Hen-ny Pen-ny flew up the chim-ney.

They went to High Dov-er and found the nest of gold-en eggs.

Norwegian Folk Tale.

73. Han-sel's Coat

Sheep: Where is your coat, lit-tle Han-sel?

It is cold this spring morn-ing.

Han-sel: I have no coat. Moth-er can-not

get me a coat till win-ter comes.

I wish I could have one now.

Sheep: I will help you, Han-sel.

Take some of my wool. There!

Now you can make a warm coat.

Han-sel: Oh, thank you! But how can I

make a coat from this curl-y wool?

Thorn Bush: Come here, Han-sel. Pull the

curl-y wool o-ver my long thorns.

They will comb it and make

it straight.

Han-sel: Oh, thank you! How straight and

soft you have made it! But this is not

a coat yet. What shall I do now?

Spi-der: Give me the wool, Han-sel.

I will spin the threads, and make

them in-to cloth for you. There it is.

Crab: What have you there, Han-sel?

Han-sel: This is cloth for a coat.

Crab: My claws are like scis-sors.

I will cut it out for you. There it is!

Han-sel: Thank you, kind Crab.

I wish I could sew.

Then I could make my coat.

Bird: I will sew your coat for you. I sew my

      nest to-geth-er ev-er-y spring. See,

      I take a thread in my beak. Then

      I pull it through and through the

      cloth. There is your coat, Han-sel.

Han-sel: Oh, thank you all!

      How hap-py moth-er will be

      to see my nice warm coat.

Folk Tale.

74. The Lamb-kin

Once up-on a time was a wee, wee Lamb-kin.

The Lamb-kin jumped a-bout on his lit-tle legs.

He ate the green grass and had a fine time.

One day he thought he would go to see his Gran-ny.

"I shall have a fine time!" he said.

"I shall have such good things to eat when I get there!"

The Lamb-kin jumped a-bout on his lit-tle legs.

He was as hap-py as he could be.

As he was go-ing a-long the road he met a jack-al.

Now the jack-al likes to eat ten-der lit-tle lamb-kins. So the jack-al said,

"Lamb-kin! Lamb-kin! I'll eat you!"

But the Lamb-kin jumped a-bout on his lit-tle legs and said,

"To Gran-ny's house I go,

Where I shall fat-ter grow;

Then you can eat me so."

The jack-al likes fat lambs, so he let Lamb-kin go on to get fat.

By and by Lamb-kin met a ti-ger.

Then he met a wolf.

Then he met a dog.

They all like good things to eat.

They like ten-der lamb-kins, so they all called out,

"Lamb-kin! Lamb-kin!

We'll eat you!"

But Lamb-kin jumped a-bout on his lit-tle legs and said,

"To Gran-ny's house I go,

Where I shall fat-ter grow;

Then you can eat me so."

The ti-ger and the wolf and the dog all like fat lamb-kins.

So they let Lamb-kin go on to his Gran-ny's to get fat.

At last Lamb-kin got to his Gran-ny's house. Gran-ny came to the door to see him.

"Oh, Gran-ny, dear!" he said. "I have prom-ised to get ver-y fat.

I must keep my prom-ise.

Please put me in-to the corn bin."

So his Gran-ny put him in-to the corn bin.

Lamb-kin stayed there sev-en days and ate and ate and ate.

At last he grew ver-y fat.

"How fat you are, Lamb-kin," said his Gran-ny.

"You must go home."

"Oh, no!" said Lamb-kin.

"The ti-ger might eat me up."

"But you must go home, Lamb-kin," said his Gran-ny.

"Well, then," said Lamb-kin,

"I will tell you what to do.

You must take a goat skin and make a lit-tle Drum-kin. I can sit in-side and roll home."

So she made a Drum-kin.

Lamb-kin got in-to it, and his Gran-ny sewed it up.

Then Lamb-kin be-gan to roll a-long the road to his home.

Soon he met the ti-ger.

The ti-ger called out,

"Drum-kin! Drum-kin!

Have you seen Lamb-kin?"

Lamb-kin, in his soft nest, called back,

"Lost in the for-est, and so are you!

On, lit-tle Drum-kin! Tum-pa, tum-too!"

The ti-ger was ang-ry. "Now I shall have no fat Lamb-kin to eat," he said.

"Why didn't I eat him when I had him?"

By and by Lamb-kin met the dog and the wolf.

They called to him,

"Drum-kin! Drum-kin!

Have you seen Lamb-kin?"

And Lamb-kin, in his soft, warm nest, called back to them,

"Lost in the for-est, and so are you!

On, lit-tle Drum-kin! Tum-pa, tum-too!"

The dog and the wolf were ver-y ang-ry be-cause they had no fat Lamb-kin to eat.

But Lamb-kin rolled a-long laugh-ing and sing-ing,

"Tum-pa, tum-too!

Tum-pa, tum-too!"

At last Lamb-kin met the jack-al, who said,

"Drum-kin! Drum-kin!

Have you seen Lamb-kin?"

Lamb-kin, in his soft nest, called back,

"Lost in the for-est, and so are you!

On, lit-tle Drum-kin! Tum-pa, tum-too!"

Now the jack-al was wise. He knew

Lamb-kin's voice. So he called out,

"Lamb-kin! Lamb-kin!

Come out of that Drum-kin!"

"Come and make me!"

shout-ed Lamb-kin.

The jack-al ran af-ter Drum-kin.

But Drum-kin rolled fast-er and fast-er,

and soon rolled a-way from him.

The last thing the jack-al heard was,

"Lost in the for-est, and so are you!

On, lit-tle Drum-kin! Tum-pa, tum-too!"

A Tale from India.

75. Snow Flakes

Child: Lit-tle white feath-ers

    Fill-ing the air—

    Lit-tle white feath-ers!

    How came you there?

Snow flakes: We came from the cloud birds,

    Fly-ing so high,

    Shak-ing their white wings

    Up in the sky.

Child: Lit-tle white feath-ers,

    Swift-ly you go!

    Lit-tle white snow flakes,

    I love you so!

Snow flakes: We are swift be-cause

    We have work to do;

    But look up at us,

    And we will kiss you.

Mary Mapes Dodge.

The Clouds

    White sheep, white sheep,

      On a blue hill,

    When the wind stops,

      You all stand still.

    When the winds blow,

      You walk a-way slow;

    White sheep, white sheep,

      Where do you go?

Christina G. Rossetti.

Appendices

Appendix A:
About the Orton-Gillingham Method

In the early decades of the 1900s, physician Samuel Orton and psychologist Anna Gillingham identified the main phonograms used to write the English language as part of their method for helping people with reading disabilities. Elementary educator Romalda Spalding, a student of Dr. Orton, later expanded upon the work of Orton and Gillingham to create the Spalding Method of teaching reading, writing, and spelling.

Many other Orton-Gillingham programs have since been developed which teach reading through spelling. The phonograms—letters or groups of letters which form sounds—represent the forty-five sounds in the English language. Children first learn the phonograms, then they begin spelling. Spelling words are marked according to phonograms and spelling rules. Amazingly, just seventy-five phonograms and thirty spelling rules can be used to explain most English words—98%, in fact. This is an incredible percentage considering that most people believe that English is not a phonetic language.

Why Write Another Orton Phonogram Reading Program?

There are plenty of Orton-Gillingham programs on the market. My main reason for writing yet another one was that I found the others difficult to implement. I am a mother with five children, and whenever it's been time to teach another child to read, I've been either pregnant, had a baby or toddler, or we were moving cross-country.

It shouldn't be surprising that busy mothers often find these programs difficult to implement at first. In the past, some of them have even required the teacher to take a class in order to be able to teach the course. Now, there are more teaching helps available, but they can be expensive.

So the first thing I wanted was something that was pick-up and go. Teaching the phonograms and dictating spelling words is actually very simple and straight forward. The second thing I wanted was a program that focused, quite simply, on the beginning reader, including a list of spelling words that led straight into an inexpensive, easy-to-find set of stories to read. These were the criteria which led to Reading Lessons Through Literature.

Why Teach the Phonograms?

There are those who argue that learning the seventy-five basic phonograms is more than what is necessary to learn to read. Technically, this is true. Children are adaptable, and their flexible little minds often learn things in spite of our teaching mistakes. I'm not arguing that it's the only way to teach reading. I'm arguing that it's the best way to teach reading, for the following reasons:

1. There is a logic to the spelling of the English language, but without learning the basic phonograms and spelling rules, the logic is difficult to see and apply. Learning to read without knowing all of the phonograms is the same as learning to read without knowing the most common sounds of the individual letters, which is to say that while it may be possible, it's far more difficult than it needs to be. With the basic phonograms and thirty spelling rules, the majority of English words can be understood and spelled. Why give children only some of the tools needed for decoding the language? Math would also seem illogical if we were never taught that each number represents a specific quantity.

2. Those who do not teach a complete phonics program which includes all of the basic phonograms often teach some sight words instead. The common list of sight words, called Dolch words because they were compiled by Dr. Dolch in 1948, includes words that can make up 50-70% of a general text. It is commonly—and erroneously—stated that many of these words cannot be sounded out and therefore must be memorized by sight.

There are 220 Dolch words, 220 words that many children are expected to memorize by sight. Why are 75 basic phonograms considered more difficult than 220 sight words?

3. When programs do not teach all the phonograms, they leave a child with no direction on how to decipher new words which have uncommon phonogram sounds.

4. Proponents of teaching a whole language (sight word heavy) reading program often make a disturbing observation. They point out that children will figure out the phonogram sounds through learning the sight words. In other words, instead of being taught, children are expected to figure it out on their own. No wonder we have a literacy problem in this country.

Comparison of O-G and Phonics Programs

The processes used to teach O-G programs and traditional phonics programs look very different, leading parents and teachers to worry that focusing on spelling as O-G does will mean that it will take a child longer to learn how to read. Although the processes are different, they do include some of the same types of activities.

Phonics programs teach a sound and then some words. Reading Lessons Through Literature and other O-G programs do the same while adding the analysis and teaching the spelling rules, which are often pronunciation rules as well. Children doing an O-G program should be reading their spelling words daily. At six, a child might learn 10-20 new words per week and might be reading 50-100 words every day. The reading practice is there, but it looks different than it does in a traditional phonics program.

Phonics programs typically recommend writing the words, too. It's more of a different way of looking at it than a completely different process. Phonics programs say to practice sounding these words and syllables out, then go write them. O-G programs say to write each sound as you hear it, then go read them.

To adults who have been reading since childhood, it can seem like reading and spelling are two different things, but to the child writing down the spelling words, spelling and reading are the same thing.

Appendix B: Prepared Dictation

After finishing all the levels of Reading Lessons Through Literature, you should be comfortable enough with the phonograms and the spelling rules to analyze any word you come across. Many people continue using this methodology to teach advanced spelling to their children.

My preferred method to continue spelling is through prepared dictation. Selections for prepared dictation are included in English Lessons Through Literature, my grammar program. However, you can do prepared dictation with any text you like.

Dictation should not begin until third or fourth grade, depending on the readiness of the child. A child who has finished Reading Lessons Through Literature but who is not yet ready for dictation could analyze words from his copywork a few times a week instead.

In prepared dictation, children type or write a passage after studying it for five to ten minutes. The basic process was described by Charlotte Mason in her book Home Education. We combine the method with analyzing words according to phonograms and spelling rules.

I know that dictation can sound like a huge, time consuming exercise, especially with multiple children. It's not. We do prepared dictation twice a week, on the "off" days from grammar. First, I try to have my boys read through the spelling rules at least once each week, and we make an effort to analyze words that illustrate the different rules. (If they don't appear naturally through the passages we study, then we occasionally spend some time exploring a rule rather than a passage.) Then, each of my boys studies his passage for about ten minutes. He chooses, sometimes with my help, two or three words to analyze. A passage should not have more than three or four unknown words to be studied, though there's nothing wrong with analyzing extra words. He adds these to his Spelling Journal, analyzing each word syllable by syllable.

The Spelling Journal organizes words according to phonogram or spelling rule, and it is a free download on my site. The Spelling Journal can help identify problem spelling areas. Also, having children read through their Spelling Journals occasionally can help reinforce lessons from their previous studies. If you prefer to avoid printing out workbooks, then you could use the Spelling Journal as a template for creating a Spelling Journal in a composition book.

Dictations may be written or typed. My boys type their dictations. The spelling and grammar checks are turned off in our word processing program, and we increase the font size to 20+ points so that I can read over their shoulders. I read the exercises while each boy takes his turn at the keyboard. I stand behind them so that I can make sure they don't make any mistakes. When a mistake is made, we correct immediately. After the dictation, we analyze, or re-analyze, the missed word. Most weeks, there are no missed words from any of my boys.

Beginners can start with just a sentence or two while older children can type or write up to several paragraphs. We use a variety of sources, including Aesop's fables, literature, Bible verses, poetry, and even my children's free reading choices. It is important to avoid passages which contain incorrect grammar, which many modern books do. However, I've found that dictation goes easier when the child is studying a passage he loves.

Appendix C: Sample Schedules

The following pages have sample schedules. The charts show a detailed day to day plan for the first twelve weeks. The lists show an overview of the progression of all three levels.

Level 1: Spelling Lists 1-29

Level 2: Spelling Lists 30-75

Level 3: Spelling Lists 76-127

The first schedules are at the regular pace for starting with younger children, approximately Kindergarten age. This pace will take three years to complete three levels. The schedule begins teaching two phonograms per day and fifteen words per week.

The second schedules are at an accelerated pace for starting with older children, approximately first grade age. This pace will take two years to complete three levels. The schedule begins teaching four phonograms per day and twenty words per week.

Keep in mind, though, that you can and should adjust the pace to make the program work for you. The schedules are only here to give a general idea of how to use the program. Reduce the number of words down to only ten per week for a child who is overwhelmed by fifteen, or dictate only three words every day for a child who is overwhelmed by the writing. Increase the number of words for a child who needs more of a challenge.

The stories are not specifically scheduled. The child may read each story when he's covered the spelling list for the story and he's comfortable reading the words, even if he's still sounding them out. That will vary from child to child.

	Monday	Tuesday	Wednesday	Thursday	Friday
1	Learn c, a Review Phonograms	Learn d, g Review Phonograms	Learn o, qu Phonogram Quiz	Learn i, j Review Phonograms	Learn m, n Phonogram Quiz
2	Learn r, l Review Phonograms	Learn h, k Review Phonograms	Learn b, p Phonogram Quiz	Learn t, u Review Phonograms	Learn y, e Phonogram Quiz
3	Learn f, s Review Phonograms	Learn v, w Review Phonograms	Learn x, z Phonogram Quiz	Learn th, ck Review Phonograms	Learn ai, ay Phonogram Quiz
4	Learn sh, ng Review Phonograms List 1-A (5 words)	Learn ee, oo Review Phonograms Read Spelling Words	Learn ou, ow Phonogram Quiz List 1-A (5 words), Read	Learn ar, ch Review Phonograms Read Spelling Words	Learn au, aw Phonogram Quiz List 1-B (5 words), Read
5	Learn oi, oy Review Phonograms List 1-B (5 words), Read	Learn er, ur Review Phonograms Read Spelling Words	Learn ir, ear Phonogram Quiz List 1-C (5 words), Read	Learn wor, wh Review Phonograms Read Spelling Words	Learn ea, or Phonogram Quiz List 1-C (5 words), Read
6	Learn ed, ew Review Phonograms List 1-D (5 words), Read	Learn cei, gu Review Phonograms Read Spelling Words	Learn wr, augh Phonogram Quiz List 1-D (5 words), Read	Learn ui, oa Review Phonograms Read Spelling Words	Learn ph, oe Phonogram Quiz List 1-E (5 words), Read

	Monday	Tuesday	Wednesday	Thursday	Friday
7	Learn tch, dge Review Phonograms List 1-E (5 words), Read	Learn ey, bu Review Phonograms Read Spelling Words	Learn ei, eigh Phonogram Quiz List 1-F (5 words), Read	Learn ci, ti Review Phonograms Read Spelling Words	Learn si, kn Phonogram Quiz List 1-F (5 words), Read
8	Learn igh, ie Review Phonograms List 1-G (5 words), Read	Learn gn, ough, mb Review Phonograms	Phonogram Quiz Read Spelling Words List 1-G (5 words)	Review Phonograms Read Spelling Words	Phonogram Quiz Read Spelling Words List 1-H (5 words)
9	Review Phonograms Read Spelling Words List 1-H (5 words)	Review Phonograms Read Spelling Words	Phonogram Quiz Read Spelling Words List 1-I (5 words)	Review Phonograms Read Spelling Words	Phonogram Quiz Read Spelling Words List 1-I (5 words)
10	Review Phonograms Read Spelling Words List 1-J (5 words)	Review Phonograms Read Spelling Words	Phonogram Quiz Read Spelling Words List 1-J (5 words)	Review Phonograms Read Spelling Words	Phonogram Quiz Read Spelling Words List 1-K (5 words)
11	Review Phonograms Read Spelling Words List 1-K (5 words)	Review Phonograms Read Spelling Words	Phonogram Quiz Read Spelling Words List 1-L (5 words)	Review Phonograms Read Spelling Words	Phonogram Quiz Read Spelling Words List 1-L (5 words)
12	Review Phonograms Read Spelling Words List 1-M (5 words)	Review Phonograms Read Spelling Words	Phonogram Quiz Read Spelling Words List 1-M (5 words)	Review Phonograms Read Spelling Words	Phonogram Quiz Read Spelling Words List 1-N (5 words)

Year 1

Week 1   Phonograms c through n

Week 2   Phonograms r through e

Week 3   Phonograms f through ay

Week 4   Phonograms sh through aw
        Spelling Lists: 1-A, half 1-B

Week 5   Phonograms oi through or
        Spelling Lists: half 1-B, 1-C

Week 6   Phonograms ed through oe
        Spelling Lists: 1-D, half 1-E

Week 7   Phonograms tch through kn
        Spelling Lists: half 1-E, 1-F

Week 8   Phonograms igh through mb
        Spelling Lists: 1-G, half 1-H

Week 9   Spelling Lists: half 1-H, 1-I

Week 10 Spelling Lists: 1-J, half 1-K

Week 11 Spelling Lists: half 1-K, 1-L

Week 12 Spelling Lists: 1-M, half 1-N

Week 13 Spelling Lists: half 1-N, 1-O

Week 14 Spelling Lists: 1-P, half 1-Q

Week 15 Spelling Lists: half 1-Q, 1-R

Week 16 Spelling Lists: 1-S, half 1-T

Week 17 Spelling Lists: half 1-T, 2

Week 18 Spelling Lists: 3, half 4

Week 19 Spelling Lists: half 4, 5

Week 20 Spelling Lists: 6, half 7

Week 21 Spelling Lists: half 7, 8

Week 22 Spelling Lists: 9, half 10

Week 23 Spelling Lists: half 10, 11

Week 24 Spelling Lists: 12, half 13

Week 25 Spelling Lists: half 13, 14

Week 26 Spelling Lists: 15, half 16

Week 27 Spelling Lists: half 16, 17

Week 28 Spelling Lists: 18, half 19

Week 29 Spelling Lists: half 19, 20

Week 30 Spelling Lists: 21, half 22

Week 31 Spelling Lists: half 22, 23

Week 32 Spelling Lists: 24, half 25

Week 33 Spelling Lists: half 25, 26

Week 34 Spelling Lists: 27, half 28

Week 35 Spelling Lists: half 28, 29

Year 2

Year 3

Week 1   Phonograms c through e

Week 2   Phonograms f through aw

Week 3   Phonograms oi through oe

Week 4   Phonograms tch through mb

           Spelling Lists: 69-70

Week 5   Spelling Lists: 71-72

Week 6   Spelling Lists: 73-74

Week 7   Spelling Lists: 75-76

Week 8   Spelling Lists: 77-78

Week 9   Spelling Lists: 79-80

Week 10 Spelling Lists: 81-82

Week 11 Spelling Lists: 83-84

Week 12 Spelling Lists: 85-86

Week 13 Spelling Lists: 87-88

Week 14 Spelling Lists: 89-90

Week 15 Spelling Lists: 91-92

Week 16 Spelling Lists: 93-94

Week 17 Spelling Lists: 95-96

Week 18 Spelling Lists: 97-98

Week 19 Spelling Lists: 99-100

Week 20 Spelling Lists: 101-102

Week 21 Spelling Lists: 103-104

Week 22 Spelling Lists: 105-106

Week 23 Spelling Lists: 107-108

Week 24 Spelling Lists: 109-110

Week 25 Spelling Lists: 111-112

Week 26 Spelling Lists: 113-114

Week 27 Spelling Lists: 115-116

Week 28 Spelling Lists: 117-118

Week 29 Spelling Lists: 119-120

Week 30 Spelling Lists: 121-122

Week 31 Spelling Lists: 123-124

Week 32 Spelling Lists: 125-126

Week 33 Spelling Lists: 127

	Monday	Tuesday	Wednesday	Thursday	Friday
1	Learn c, a, d, g	Learn o, qu, i, j Review Phonograms	Learn m, n, r, l Phonogram Quiz	Learn h, k, b, p Review Phonograms	Learn t, u, y, e Phonogram Quiz
2	Learn f, s, v, w Review Phonograms	Learn x, z, th, ck Review Phonograms	Learn ai, ay, sh, ng Phonogram Quiz	Learn ee, oo, ou, ow Review Phonograms	Learn ar, ch, au, aw Phonogram Quiz
3	Learn oi, oy, er, ur Review Phonograms	Learn ir, ear, wor, wh Review Phonograms	Learn ea, or, ed, ew Phonogram Quiz	Learn cei, gu, wr, augh Review Phonograms	Learn ui, oa, ph, oe Phonogram Quiz
4	Learn tch, dge, ey, bu Review Phonograms	Learn ei, eigh, ci, ti Review Phonograms List 1-A	Learn si, kn, igh, ie Phonogram Quiz Read Spelling Words	Learn gn, ough, mb Review Phonograms List 1-B	Phonogram Quiz Read Spelling Words
5	Review Phonograms Read Spelling Words	Review Phonograms List 1-C	Phonogram Quiz Read Spelling Words	Review Phonograms List 1-D	Phonogram Quiz Read Spelling Words
6	Review Phonograms Read Spelling Words	Review Phonograms List 1-E	Phonogram Quiz Read Spelling Words	Review Phonograms List 1-F	Phonogram Quiz Read Spelling Words

	Monday	Tuesday	Wednesday	Thursday	Friday
7	Review Phonograms Read Spelling Words	Review Phonograms List 1-G	Phonogram Quiz Read Spelling Words Phonogram Quiz	Review Phonograms List 1-H Review Phonograms	Phonogram Quiz Read Spelling Words Phonogram Quiz
8	Review Phonograms Read Spelling Words	Review Phonograms List 1-I	Read Spelling Words	Read Spelling Words List 1-J	Read Spelling Words
9	Review Phonograms Read Spelling Words	Review Phonograms Read Spelling Words List 1-K	Phonogram Quiz Read Spelling Words	Review Phonograms Read Spelling Words List 1-L	Phonogram Quiz Read Spelling Words
10	Review Phonograms Read Spelling Words	Review Phonograms Read Spelling Words List 1-M	Phonogram Quiz Read Spelling Words	Review Phonograms Read Spelling Words List 1-N	Phonogram Quiz Read Spelling Words
11	Review Phonograms Read Spelling Words	Review Phonograms Read Spelling Words List 1-O	Phonogram Quiz Read Spelling Words	Review Phonograms Read Spelling Words List 1-P	Phonogram Quiz Read Spelling Words
12	Review Phonograms Read Spelling Words	Review Phonograms Read Spelling Words List 1-Q	Phonogram Quiz Read Spelling Words	Review Phonograms Read Spelling Words List 1-R	Phonogram Quiz Read Spelling Words

Year 1

Week 1   Phonograms c through e

Week 2   Phonograms f through aw

Week 3   Phonograms oi through oe

Week 4   Phonograms tch through mb

Spelling Lists: 1-A, 1-B

Week 5   Capitals c through e

Spelling Lists: 1-C, 1-D

Week 6   Capitals f through z

Spelling Lists: 1-E, 1-F

Week 7   Spelling Lists: 1-G, 1-H

Week 8   Spelling Lists: 1-I, 1-J

Week 9   Spelling Lists: 1-K, 1-L

Week 10 Spelling Lists: 1-M, 1-N

Week 11 Spelling Lists: 1-O, 1-P

Week 12 Spelling Lists: 1-Q, 1-R

Week 13 Spelling Lists: 1-S, 1-T

Week 14 Spelling Lists: 2-3

Week 15 Spelling Lists: 4-5

Week 16 Spelling Lists: 6-7

Week 17 Spelling Lists: 8-9

Week 18 Spelling Lists: 10-11

Week 19 Spelling Lists: 12-13

Week 20 Spelling Lists: 14-15

Week 21 Spelling Lists: 16-17

Week 22 Spelling Lists: 18-19

Week 23 Spelling Lists: 20-21

Week 24 Spelling Lists: 22-23

Week 25 Spelling Lists: 24-25

Week 26 Spelling Lists: 26-27

Week 27 Spelling Lists: 28-29

Week 28 Spelling Lists: 30-31

Week 29 Spelling Lists: 32-33

Week 30 Spelling Lists: 34-35

Week 31 Spelling Lists: 36-37

Week 32 Spelling Lists: 38-39

Week 33 Spelling Lists: 40-41

Week 34 Spelling Lists: 42-43

Week 35 Spelling Lists: 44-45

Week 36 Spelling Lists: 46-47

Year 2

Appendix D: Glossary of Spelling Words

This list of spelling words is in alphabetical order and shows in which lesson each word is analyzed. Lists 1-29 are in Level 1, lists 30-75 are in Level 2, lists 76-127 are in Level 3, and lists 128-173 are in Level 4.

Spelling Words in Alphabetical Order

Spelling Words in Alphabetical Order

Spelling Words in Alphabetical Order

Spelling Words in Alphabetical Order

Spelling Words in Alphabetical Order

Made in the USA
Lexington, KY
26 February 2018